Facing the City

For my mother and to the
memory of my father and sister

Facing the City

Urban Mission in the 21st Century

Rod Garner

EPWORTH PRESS

Scripture quotations are from the New Revised Standard
Version of the Bible, copyright 1989 by the Division of
Christian Education of the National Council of the Churches
of Christ in the USA. Used by permission. All rights reserved.

British Library Cataloguing in Publication data

A catalogue record for this book is available
from the British Library

0716 0580 7

First published in 2004
by Epworth Press
4 John Wesley Road
Werrington
Peterborough PE4 7ZP

Typeset by Regent Typesetting, London
Printed and bound in Great Britain by
Biddles Ltd, www.biddles.co.uk

Contents

Foreword

Within a week of writing this Foreword, I hope to be present when a new Church Commission on Urban Life and Faith is launched. Twenty years on from the publication of *Faith in the City*, this fresh initiative plans to review what has been achieved and where we find ourselves in city and Church. As a member of the Archbishop's Commission that produced that report, I find Rod Garner's new book both encouraging and challenging. *Facing the City* should be a very useful tool for the commission. Rod Garner quotes with approval Lord Scarman's description of *Faith in the City*: 'It will take its place, I believe, as a classic description of one of the most serious troubles in British society.' *Faith in the City* saw a nation confronted by 'a grave and fundamental injustice in the cities'.

In *Facing the City*, Garner faces the city with reality, yet with vigorous hopefulness. That spirit of hope bubbles up out of his life of worship, both personal and corporate. He makes the fair criticism of *Faith in the City* that it gave too small a place to worship. *Facing the City* insists on the importance of worship that can 'praise open' the future. 'A coherent and cohesive sense of Christian identity becomes more and not less important in the context where we are all now cosmopolitan citizens.' This is underlined by my own experience in helping bring together conversations between Christians, Jews and Muslims in Liverpool. Those Jews and Muslims we met with would not be impressed by Christians, if we had pretended that there was nothing distinctive about our faith. They and we brought full-blooded beliefs to the dialogue, together with a profound respect for those who brought their deep convictions too. And reaching out into that cosmopolitan world of the city touches our worship too: 'As urban culture evolves with its amalgam of new experiences and questions, so too are new aspects and features of Jesus discovered.'

I saw Rod Garner at work in parishes in Liverpool Diocese. He also writes out of first-hand experience of serving a struggling congregation in Hull, which grew in five years of hard and imaginative work from eight members to rather more than thirty. He tells the human stories, both comic and tragic, that bring the parish to life to the reader. No one method of ministry is held up as 'successful', but inner-city parishes can and do move beyond survival to reach out into the community. The vision of the Church is not simply of a 'gathered congregation', but of a springboard for mission – being sent out 'to love and serve the Lord' among our neighbours.

Garner reads a lot – theology, poetry, novels, sociology and history – that enriches the picture of today's city. As Lay Training Officer in the East Riding of York Diocese and Diocesan Theological Consultant since returning to Liverpool Diocese nine years ago, he has engaged with many clergy and lay people on these issues. He shares the fruits of his reading, seeking to bring that down to the local.

In the last 20 years we have needed to recognize the influences of globalization. Decisions taken far away alter lives, and peoples who were once divided by oceans now live in the next street. The scale of a great city sometimes seems inhuman and threatening. Garner shows that it can be life-enhancing too: 'Whatever the urban landscape represents in terms of money or danger, it is at the same time a place of conviviality, where individuals and groups meet, trade, exchange concerns and ideas.' Understanding our interconnectedness helps us grasp what is going in.

Rod Garner was involved in the follow-up to *Faith in the City*, meeting with groups in the wider community. He shows how Church Urban Fund grants have helped parishes to turn outwards to serve the wider community. He observed an old Anglican caution that was readier to engage in pastoral work rather than addressing the deep-seated issues of powerlessness and political marginalization which the report had raised. 'A theology of the Kingdom, with its challenge to institutions as well as individuals has proved less palatable – partly out of human disinclination to face the disturbing social implications, and then again as a consequence of belonging to a national Church that at the local level still regards civility, stability and compassion as epitomizing English Christianity.'

At the same time, Garner takes issue with those critics who are needlessly cynical about governments. He sees Old Testament prophets using words both of judgement and of promise, and, with William Temple, he says that, notwithstanding a tendency to sinfulness, human institutions are still worthy of endorsement because they are integral to the creation. And churches can properly work in collaboration with good government policies, without becoming their tools. Some years ago, I led a delegation of Church leaders to see Michael Howard, then Secretary of State for the Environment. We were protesting that the Government's Urban Programme was being withdrawn, without the Churches or the Voluntary Movement – often praised by the Government as being vital allies – being alerted. One of our party said to Mr Howard, 'You need us. There are many estates on which we maintain the only presence sustaining hope.' The partnership with government agencies can and should be a robust one.

Facing the City shows the strength of local ecumenical partnerships. Partnership is a key word, if the Church is to bring its vision and care effectively to bear in the community. Partners, who may belong to other churches, other faiths or none, can become trusted allies. Comparatively small numbers in churches can be significant players in tackling needs.

This is a book to make all of us who care about the long-standing struggle of the churches to root themselves effectively in urban priority areas think afresh. It has made me think again with renewed hope.

David Sheppard
January 2004

Acknowledgements

T. S. Eliot, 'Choruses from the Rock 1934', in *The Complete Poems and Plays of T. S. Eliot*, Faber & Faber, 1969.

Jon McGregor, *If nobody speaks of remarkable things*, Bloomsbury, 2002.

'The Prophet's Speech', in *Words from the Late Late, Service*, Sticky Music Glasgow, 1993.

Abbreviations

CBAC	Committee on Black Anglican Concerns
CMC	Churches Main Committee
COPEC	Conference on Christian Politics, Economics and Citizenship
CPAG	Child Poverty Action Group
CSU	Christian Social Union
CUF	Church Urban Fund
ICRC	Inner Cities Religious Council
IMF	International Monetary Fund
SRB	Single Regeneration Budget
UPA	Urban Priority Area

Introduction

By a happy coincidence this book appears shortly before the twenty-fifth anniversary of my ordination as a priest in the Church of England. I have spent these years in urban communities combining the work of parish ministry with a varied remit as a theological educator. The book has been written amid the cares, joys and responsibilities of parish life and represents the stance of one urban practitioner. It is offered as a contribution to the perennial and now increasingly urgent debate concerning how Christian theology responds to the signs of the times. Over the years two issues among others have preoccupied me: the changing role of the churches in the city and the need to understand the forces shaping our urban experience in the new millennium. Simply carrying on carrying on is, I believe, no longer a viable urban strategy for local congregations. Fresh thinking is called for that needs to be grounded in worship and prayer and a readiness to learn from a Christian past that can still encourage us today.

In Part Three I offer a number of practical suggestions that I hope will contribute to the renewal of urban churches and their communities. I have tried to keep one eye on present and future developments and with the other I have looked back. As a teenager I was deeply influenced by my local vicar – one of those quiet saints who wrote no books but left an indelible mark on the lives he touched. I became involved in his ministry to the poor and homeless and saw with my own eyes what it meant to be down and out. Years later I realized that his concern owed much to the compassionate and costly witness of the churches that began in the slums of nineteenth-century England. I find this tradition morally persuasive and because our experience of the present is always being shaped by what has gone before (often in ways that we barely comprehend) my hope is that others will be moved by the characters and events that permeate the opening chapters, in Part One. Here I am thinking particularly of the Archbishop's Commission on Urban Priority Areas that led in 1985 to the publication of *Faith in the City* – arguably the most socially significant report of the Church of England in the last century. Almost 20 years on this is a good moment to assess its relevance for urban mission when, as Part Two will show, today's cities still constitute a formidable context for faith and practice.

I also want to celebrate the urban. We are told so often about its drawbacks and dangers that it becomes easy to overlook the creative possibilities that exist within its boundaries for human flourishing. I was born and raised close to the heart of Manchester and retain the vivid memories of a small boy and youth mesmerized by its sights and sounds. Since then I have travelled to some of the world's biggest cities and continue to be fascinated by their energy and inventiveness. On a smaller scale I have also come to recognize the urban as a place of gift where intimations of that elusive kingdom proclaimed by Jesus are to be found. Something more than reports and sober analysis is required to convey all of this and in what follows readers will find stories, poetry and philosophical reflections alongside the more prosaic facts and figures unearthed by my research. Underlying the book is a conviction that despite the enormous challenges confronting the urban church, local congregations can survive and make a positive difference in a world that in the aftermath of September 11, 2001, has assumed new and frightening dimensions.

The poet W. H. Auden reminds us that our last thoughts should be thanks. I would like to acknowledge the generous financial assistance I received from the Ecclesiastical Insurance Group, the Josephine Butler Trust and the Diocese of Liverpool towards my research. The Rt Revd Donald Snelgrove, formerly

Bishop of Hull, the Ven. Bob Metcalfe, former Archdeacon of Liverpool, and Lord David Sheppard, former Bishop of Liverpool, were all instrumental in securing these grants and I gladly thank them for their support. My own approach to urban mission bears the imprint of other lives. At the outset I was taught the importance of learning to be still and the discipline of daily prayer by my College Principal, Revd Dr Anthony Bird and Fr John Gordon, vicar of St Paul's, Birkenhead, and, for two important years, my senior parish colleague. Fr John Walker, who died in 2000, was not only a dear friend but also a stimulating conversation partner with a heart for the city and a probing mind that kept my own alert. Since returning to Merseyside I have been privileged to collaborate with Professor Hilary Russell of John Moores University: somehow she has always managed to secure the information I need or point me in the right direction. Professor Elaine Graham supervised my research at Manchester University and again proved a valuable and valued mentor. Canon John Atherton of Manchester Cathedral cleared my path at a critical juncture and I shall always be grateful for his wisdom, guidance and encouragement. I wish to thank my former parish administrator, Ruby Smith, who overcame initial and quite understandable reservations (in view of my handwriting!) and took on the tasks of word processing and proofreading with commendable competence and good will. And special thanks to Christine, my partner down all the days, for the patience and perseverance she brought to the processing of the earlier PhD manuscript. Assuredly, a labour of love.

Part One

The Word Made Concrete

1 Patterns of Urban Mission:
A Critical Retrospective

The Nineteenth-Century Background

Foreign visitors to England during the early years of the nineteenth century were confronted by the contrast between affluence and poverty, particularly in London, conspicuously the wealthiest city in the world. On 8 November 1816, John Quincy Adams, an American diplomat, encountered a weary man in the street who told him he had not eaten for two days. 'The number of these wretched objects I meet in my daily work is distressing', he noted.

> Not a day passes but we have beggars come to the house, each with a different, hideous tale of misery. The extremes of opulence and wont are more remarkable and more constantly obvious in this country than in any other that I ever saw.[1]

Four years later another visitor, this time an artist, experienced similar harsh encounters. Théodore Géricault (1791–1824) committed them to canvas; his drawings represented a compendium of suffering and squalor in the midst of a modern metropolis. Disenchantment best described the condition of the poor. They knew little beyond the daily grind and struggle and the burden of economic exploitation by the powerful.

As this tide of human misery continued to flow into the new industrial cities, it became increasingly evident that the Church as the nation's wealthiest institution was failing in its duty to the most needy. Writing his official report on the 1851 religious census, the Anglican barrister Horace Mann contended that, among other reasons, clergy indifference and missionary indolence accounted for the alienation of the working class from religious institutions.[2] There is some truth in Mann's analysis. Even now it is shocking to learn that the Archbishop of Canterbury (on today's terms) received in excess of £700,000 by way of annual remuneration. Clergy were too often seen as well fed and reactionary. In 1832 all the bishops voted against the Great Reform Bill and many clergy magistrates were viewed as 'the long arm' of the Government.[3] It is also undoubtedly the case that some clergy failed to identify themselves with their parishioners. The predictable issues of education, class and lifestyle served to keep them apart and sometimes clergy were simply unperceptive in relation to the social conditions surrounding them. One curate in the 1840s was astonished to learn that there were 13 brothels within 100 yards of his home – a fact he eventually gleaned from police reports.[4] In this respect Edward Norman comments that it was 'characteristic of the upper or middle-class clergy of the Church that they sometimes attempted to acquire their knowledge of social conditions not from the evidence of their experiences but from newspapers and official reports'.[5]

Quite apart from the chasm arising out of rigid social stratification, it is also crucial to note just how frightful and dangerous were the conditions in the slum parishes. Essential services conducive to health, safety and sanitation were stretched to breaking point. Fever and disease decimated thousands. To the inhabitants it was hell on earth and hardly better to those looking on. The opportunity of living healthy and decent lives in these wretched situations was severely limited. People were inhabiting conditions which 'made it almost impossible for them to be moral much less religious'.[6] It is not surprising that clergy were sometimes reluctant to serve in such areas and that when they did they found the degradation and filth unending and unbearable.

The record of this period is not entirely bleak. There is also evidence of good and productive work discharged by the parish clergy for the sake of the poor. Clothing Clubs and Mutual Benefit Societies proliferated from the 1820s; clergy served as local organizers of philanthropic bodies and were well represented on hospital governing bodies. They were frequently reminded of the centrality of caring for the poor in their ministry[7] and 'in the undramatic circumstances of their parishes, most were responsible for the alleviation of a great deal of suffering'.[8] They did not, however, have a monopoly on compassion. Churches were frequently outnumbered by chapels, and there is some truth in G. M. Trevelyan's claim that 'Wesley's Methodism became the religion of the neglected poor'.[9] If large numbers of the urban working class remained obdurately outside the fold of organized religion – whether church or chapel – many had cause to be grateful for the personal witness and practical charity of local societies and itinerant preachers who persisted through poverty 'amidst the dark parishes of what, but for their instrumentality, would scarcely be a Christian England'.[10]

From the 1830s onwards something new began to emerge in the towns and cities. As before, there was a pastoral commitment to the downtrodden urban areas but aligned to this was a resolve to understand the plight of the poor and when necessary to speak for them. In some instances clergy assumed a more radical posture insisting that society should no longer tolerate open sewers and fever-ridden tenements. Better houses were needed along with better drainage. Bishop Walsham How remarked in 1884 on the impressive work being done by the clergy to improve working-class housing in their parishes. In the following year, Parliament implemented the 'Houses of the Working Classes Act' – legislation that had previously received a great deal of clerical support.[11]

How should we account for this shift in pastoral emphasis, and what are its distinctive features? In some cases younger clergy were influenced by the Oxford Movement and its morally strenuous ideals.[12] With impressive zeal and devotion they ministered in the slums wearing 'poverty as a cloak and lived the life of the suffering and the destitute'.[13] Elsewhere Methodist voices were moved to protest against the iniquities of the workhouses, the excessive working hours in the factories and the relentlessness of the factory owners, many of whom embraced double standards – on the one hand affirming the worth and dignity of the working classes for they were held to be made in God's image and, on the other, frequently treating them abominably. Children walked as much as 30 miles each day behind their industrial machines, and factory inspectors routinely noted the familiar debilitating illnesses of pneumonia, bronchitis, asthma, as well as kidney and stomach disorders that could all be summed up in two words – 'long hours'. All of this was contrary to Scripture and the emphasis of Christianity on the institutions of marriage and family and the need to temper the harshness of life with compassion. Richard Oastler, the steward of a large country estate in Yorkshire initiated the Ten Hours Campaign that eventually in 1850 limited the hours worked by women and children to ten hours a day. His friend Joseph Rayner Stephens inveighed against the immorality of the Poor Law that provided workhouses across the nation where the destitute with no other options left to them barring starvation were segregated by gender and often treated cruelly by local Boards of Governors.[14] The consciences of both men were affronted by such abuses that denied the word of the living God. Stephens in particular was clear where the priorities of ministry lay:

> Let the priesthood become a real ministry for the poor, not confined to the Church and the sickroom, but operating on the daily life of the poor. To reclaim the vicious, to counsel the improvident, to raise new hopes in the desponding, to be the friend and benefactor of all, is a noble mission. To instruct and relieve the poor is more God-like than to minister to the rich.[15]

As they campaigned throughout 1836 and 1837, a young Anglican priest was working on a series of letters to a Quaker friend that was to become a major theological work. *The Kingdom of Christ* by Frederick Denison Maurice was published in 1838 and his way of thinking about social issues was to prove enormously influential within the Church throughout the century and beyond.[16] On the one hand he rejected economic competition and excessive individualism as a way of life and, on the other, advocated the co-operative ideal that men should become 'Fellow workers instead of rivals' through the fostering of 'the old feeling that trades are brotherhoods'.[17]

Unlike Stephens, Maurice was no revolutionary bent on changing the system. His vision hovered between the moral and the mystical, fuelled by the conviction that human lives were not meant for sterile misery. There was also an optimism and hint of daring human possibilities in his theology that distinguished it from the prevailing evangelicalism of the day premised on the Fall, human sinfulness and the need to rescue perishing souls. In contrast to a gospel of the cross and human depravity tempered by the 'blast of judgement and the sweetness of promise',[18] Maurice emphasized the centrality of the incarnation, the goodness of creation and the inherent fellowship of Christian faith revealed in the sacraments of baptism and Eucharist. The earthly city is to be lived in not escaped from: here below the kingdom of Christ is already in existence and all 'is fused together by the spiritual power which exists for each, the minister of all, the creature of none'.[19]

From his lectures and preaching emerged a social critique that addressed the issues of sweated labour, poor sanitation, the abuse of working children and the effects of harsh employers. Many practical achievements were also linked to his name. Chris Bryant comments:

> The Industrial and Provident Societies Act of 1852, the legalising of peaceful picketing and the trades unions, the development of the Co-operative Union, the establishment of the working men's college are all directly attributable to the Christian Socialists. Indeed, if one includes the influence of Maurice on both Ruskin and Octavia Hill, the incipient

environmentalist movement of the late nineteenth century
and the National Trust itself have their origins in early
Christian Socialism.[20]

Maurice's thought marked an important transition and
came to be identified with the Guild of St Matthew (1877).
Notwithstanding its small membership, eccentricities and
internal dissensions, the guild effectively promoted the cause
of sacramentalism and the study of social and political questions from a radical theological perspective. In wishing to
change fundamentally the basis of society it proposed to unite
with socialists of every kind 'in their endeavour to seize the
state and use it for the well-being of the masses instead of the
classes'.[21] Much of the guild's influence can be attributed to
its founder Stewart Headlam. Like Maurice before him, he
was an incarnationalist and believed that all were already in
Christ. Whereas evangelicalism preached a 'two-cities' gospel
that separated the material order from the spiritual realm,
Headlam readily affirmed the secular as a place of brotherhood
where values inimical to the gospel had to be abolished.[22]

Not surprisingly, the guild's overtly political mantras made
little practical headway in the Church. But in its insistence that
Christian precepts should be brought to bear on the social and
economic conditions of the poor, the guild was the natural
precursor to the Christian Social Union (CSU) formed in 1889
that would forever be associated with the talismanic names
of Holland, Westcott and Gore. The CSU had three specific
purposes:

1 To claim for the Christian Law the ultimate authority to
  rule social practice.
2 To study in common how to apply the moral truths and
  principles of Christianity to the social and economic diffi-
  culties of the present time.
3 To present Christ in practical life as the Living Master and
  King, the enemy of wrong and selfishness, the power of
  righteousness and love.[23]

All three resolutions implied a commitment to a moral society lived in co-operation rather than competition. The resolve to study was not for its own sake but to make possible informed social action. Holland was a realist and hard facts were not to be evaded: 'There must be direct positive social results which follow on the application of the Word of Christ to the facts before us – to the Society of which we form a part. The CSU stands for nothing if not for this.'[24] He also practised what he preached, immersing himself in the inner city of London and establishing a settlement house in Hoxton that he supported for many years. Despite its genuine commitment to radical ideas the CSU could not entirely escape the charge of being elitist and paternalistic. Its leaders, after all, were from the middle and upper echelons of society with an instinctive preference for reform over revolution. But they were also charismatic and their preaching gave to the union the status of a visionary endeavour or cause, the strength and attractiveness of which was fostered, paradoxically, by its very imprecision. Describing Westcott's inaugural address at the CSU, Holland remarked: 'We pledged ourselves, we committed ourselves, we were ready to die for the cause, but if you asked us why, and for what, we could not tell you.'[25] The same kind of remark could equally have been made in relation to the sermons of Maurice and his friend Charles Kingsley, vicar of Eversley in Hampshire – a romantic idealist and born preacher capable equally of great imagination and perplexing vagueness.[26]

Despite this lack of clarity one thing at least was clear: the Church was no longer to be understood as an end in itself or as a reactionary force upholding the law. As a servant of the kingdom of God, the Church was now required to affirm the diversity of the world and also recognize that it could not go on 'treating the poor merely as poor'.[27] The alert social conscience that led to the formation of the CSU also led in the same year to the notable publication of *Lux Mundi*.[28] Michael Ramsey has described this collection of essays as 'a new era in Anglican thought . . . with the incarnation as the key to

the rationality and unity of the world'.[29] Maurice was the
harbinger of this new way of thinking and it was the particular
achievement of Westcott, Holland and Gore that the theology
of *Lux Mundi* was able to engage so effectively with the social
questions of the time.[30]

As these Christian gentlemen pondered the logic of the
incarnation and its implications for social action, the Salvation Army was also taking radical steps in its attitude to
the destitute. Social relief was no longer to be directed solely
to the 'deserving poor' but the poor: tramps, discharged prisoners, waifs and strays, prostitutes and addicts. The first depot
for food and shelter was opened at Limehouse in 1888. Two
years later, William Booth's most famous book *In Darkest
England and the Way Out* was published. It alerted Victorian
society to the existence of a jungle in England with 'a tenth of
the people living below the level of human beings'.[31] In the city
of London alone, 30,000 were prostitutes. In the previous
year, 2,297 forlorn souls committed suicide; 2,157 were found
dead on streets and in hovels; 160,000 were convicted of
drunkenness. Whatever objections polite society had to the
army's methods or its beliefs mattered little to Booth,
provided it recognized its obligation to assist him in his God-
given task of caring for the lost and perishing multitudes. As a
tract for the times his message was heard and heeded with the
public donating £100,000 in response. It also demonstrated
just how far Booth had travelled following his conversion at
a Methodist revival in 1844 and his subsequent passion for
saving souls. The social dimensions of the gospel were
undeniable and it became clear to him that Christian duty to
one's neighbour entailed more than the duty to convert him.
Soup and soap now mattered as much as salvation.

Booth was writing in the aftermath of the London dock
strike of 1889, a year which had seen not only the publication
of *Lux Mundi* but also a series of sermons by the radical
Methodist minister Hugh Price Hughes. Under the title
Social Christianity[32] he took issue with the religious and social
complacency that stultified chapel and society alike:

How do you expect virtue and morality from people living in one room? . . . a harlot is dying in a back slum . . . That harlot is as dear to Christ as the Queen of England herself . . . Let us once realise the sacredness of every human being however poor, however ignorant, however degraded and tyranny becomes impossible, lust becomes impossible, war becomes impossible.[33]

In his concern for the poor, this passionate Nonconformist preacher found an unexpected ally in the Roman Catholic Archbishop of Westminster, Cardinal Henry Manning. A convert from the Church of England and a former devotee of Newman, the Cardinal was only too painfully aware of the innumerable wretched lives that lay concealed in the lanes and alleys of Westminster Abbey and he still remembered his earlier experiences as a priest in the slum parish of Bayswater. Like Hughes he challenged his congregations to examine their consciences and acknowledge the ghettos. He did more than preach: his crucial intervention in the dock strike established him as a true champion of the working class and enabled a hitherto subdued Roman Catholicism to play a more prominent role in the life of the nation. Two years later he exerted a vital influence on the papal encyclical *Rerum Novarum*, which argued for shorter working hours, the value of trades unions and wages based on an element of 'natural justice'. He did not live long after its publication but he would have rejoiced to know that this document, arguably more than any other, was to shape the future of Catholic social teaching.

These diverse writings constituted a new theological trajectory. They pointed variously to the vital relationship between Christianity and the material world, the duty laid upon the Church to reach out to the poor, and the challenge in the name of Christ to 'seek first the Kingdom of God and his righteousness' (Matt. 6.33). In a turbulent century when the institutions and leaders of organized religion had too frequently been the targets of cynicism and complaint, they gave the churches a renewed integrity, setting the mysteries of eternity in the practicalities and problems of daily life. No less importantly, they kept intact the historical development of Christianity as an urban religion that is traceable to the early communities established by St Paul[34] and ensured that the city remained a significant theatre for service and mission.

The declaration of social principles as a fundamental Christian duty gained near unanimity among Church leaders after 1900. The Archbishop of Canterbury, Randall Davidson, a cautious and considered prelate, noted:

> It is in my judgement most important that the Church should give visible evidence that its thoughts are not concentrated simply upon matters ordinarily known as ecclesiastical, but that we are always keen, and never more keen than now, to set forward the things which make for righteousness, sobriety, and true progress in the nation's life and well-being.[35]

Five years later he was looking forward to the end of poverty within two generations. Though less clear about the means whereby principles gave way to practice – 'I can see no obvious or simple road' – the crucial point was – 'but that there is a road, and a Christian road, I am sure'.[36] Similar pronouncements came from elsewhere in the hierarchy: Winnington Ingram signalled his elevation to the see of London by requiring a denunciation of slum properties to be read in all his parish churches.[37] Cosmo Gordon Lang spoke of the 'disparity between great wealth and appalling squalor'.[38] These were not idle sentiments: years at Stepney had given him some real insight into the impoverished working class and he would have had no difficulty in endorsing a later declaration by Frank Weston to the Anglo-Catholic Congress in 1923 that his audience had no claim 'to worship Jesus in the Tabernacle if they did not pity Jesus in the slum'.[39]

The adoption of these radical social ideals by Church leaders as the twentieth century unfolded reflected their continuing growth and influence among a younger generation of theologians and social activists. The CSU undoubtedly contributed to this flourishing and the comments of sympathizers and detractors alike indicated that its moral *gravitas* touched hearts and minds. Ruth Kenyon, for example, writing in 1932 with the benefit of hindsight remarked how the CSU had transformed the outlook of a whole generation of ordinands and provided a nucleus of lay people with a social conscience.[40] Even the socialist firebrand Conrad Noel, for all his criticisms of the organization, recognized its value in convincing churchgoers of the importance of social questions.[41]

Later commentators have not been so kind. Edward Norman has criticized the vicarious aspect of much of the Church's social moralism of the period in question.[42] In a similar vein, Adrian Hastings comes close to satire in his evocation of an era characterized by a shallow commendation of socialism by clergy who would have shrunk from any real attempt at socialist reform.[43] Both criticisms have some validity yet they overlook the costly witness of clergy and congregations across the denominations who were improving the material conditions of the very poor. The famous words of Frank Weston referred to earlier reflected a moral conviction that was already being expressed through local churches.[44] And at the level of social teaching it cannot be doubted that there was a genuine concern to interpret issues like unemployment, homelessness and poverty in the light of the incarnation. In this respect the Conference on Christian Politics, Economics and Citizenship (COPEC) held in Birmingham in April 1924 represented a watershed.

The conference was just a week's duration but as an ecumenical venture its significance lay in the extensive preparation[45] and the research it initiated into Christian social attitudes. The official statistics look impressive even today: 1,500 delegates, 80 visitors from overseas churches and a COPEC council of 300. The excitement was palpable: Miss Lucy Gardner, one of the two organizing secretaries, was 'so overwhelmed by the event that on the first night of the Conference she fell out of bed in a sort of delirium'.[46] An over-

seas delegate in a more restrained way commented that
COPEC had given a new word to the English language.[47] A
week of intense discussion led delegates to approve a 'Message
of Conference' that stated:

> We have realised with a fresh intensity the scandal to our
> civilization and religion involved in the fact that thousands
> of our fellow-countrymen are without decent homes, are
> without work, are without education that would develop
> their faculties to the full.[48]

Twelve reports had been considered before this message was
issued, beginning with the *Nature of God and His Purpose for
the World* and concluding with *Historical Illustrations of the
Social Effects of Christianity*. In between, matters as diverse as
education, home life, crime, international relations and war
served to illustrate COPEC's chief concern that 'the constitution of society, the upbringing of children, national and international politics, in fact all human relationships must be
tested in the light of Christian principles'.[49]

COPEC inspired a generation with a body of ideas and
attitudes reflecting a concern for the common good. In the
words of William Temple, whose ascendancy in the Church of
England for the next two decades was confirmed by COPEC,
it enabled 'many Christian folk to think seriously about these
things who had never dreamed of doing so before'.[50] One very
young man present at the conference was the gifted son of a
teetotal, disciplined Wesleyan family in Wandsworth. Donald
Soper was 21 with an earnest temperament and a fairly conservative theology. Two years after COPEC he started work at
the South London Mission. Ten years later in 1936 he became
Superintendent of the West London Mission where he
remained for 42 years, ministering to alcoholics, prostitutes
and the homeless and gaining a controversial reputation as a
preacher and pacifist.[51] This lifelong commitment to the city
and his resolve to 'pray, give and work' for peace, social
equality and the redistribution of wealth had their genesis in

the formative influence of COPEC and its significance across the denominations.

The years following COPEC were to prove extremely hard for the ordinary people of the nation. In the aftermath of the Depression millions were unemployed[52] and in the great conurbations many were still living in appalling conditions. The Church did not hide its face. In 1933, as part of the celebrations to mark the centenary of the beginning of the Oxford Movement, the Archbishop made a plea for the abolition of the slums and better housing.[53] Bishop Garbett wrote *The Challenge of the Slums*; it was a call to action and Garbett (who himself had inspired tremendous work in South London) urged clergy to remedy the evils of poor housing in their own parishes. Important practical steps followed. Charles Jenkinson, vicar of the parish of St John and St Barnabas in Leeds assumed control of the council's Housing Committee and very quickly demolished back-to-back houses at the rate of 3,000 a year. The COPEC housing scheme in Birmingham continued vigorously; in Bristol there was a Church Tenant Association; and in Somers Town, Basil Jellicoe and the St Pancras House Improvement Society worked diligently for many years.

Unemployment had similar consequences. It was not just the loss of income and the corollary of being unable to provide for one's own needs and the needs of others that represented social evils but also the sense of exclusion from the mainstream of life. William Temple, with typical clarity, saw this all too well, particularly the less obvious and long-term implications of life on the dole:

> The worst evil . . . is creating in the unemployed a sense that they have fallen out of the common life. However much their physical needs may be supplied . . . the gravest part of their trouble remains; they are not wanted . . . Nothing will touch the real need except to enable the man to do something which is needed by the community. For it is part of the principle of personality that we should live for one another.[54]

This concern was made tangible in 1938 with the publication of *Men without Work,* a 450-page report on unemployment by the Pilgrim Trust. Temple brought various luminaries together and their collective wisdom demonstrated that the Church was capable of making a genuinely professional contribution to a major social issue based on its own theological competence and the expertise of others. *Men without Work* carefully delineated the boundaries of its subject and brought an impressive array of brains to bear upon it. And by being very specific it made a lasting contribution.

The dominance of the social radicalism attending these initiatives became less pronounced following Temple's unexpected death in 1944. In 1956, Michael Ramsey, Bishop of Durham, and later Archbishop of Canterbury, commented: 'The tradition of thought about the bearing of Christian Faith upon the problems of society has not in recent years been conspicuous within the Church of England.'[55]

In seeking an explanation for this lapse, it is necessary to recognize that it was never going to be easy to replace the vision, drive, acumen and energy embodied in Temple's leadership – the talents and qualities that had infused the heart and mind of his church and won the respect of so many outside it. His successor, Geoffrey Fisher, had no claims to theological or political wisdom, preferring instead common sense as the source of his ministry. The revision of canon law, rather than high causes, preoccupied him throughout his 16 years of office.[56] He was also a safe candidate – gifted as an administrator but entirely lacking Temple's concern for social justice. Many had thought that George Bell, the Bishop of Chichester, was the natural successor to Temple: Bell, more than any other of the bishops, had insisted on Christian ethical standards during the war and had spoken out against the consequences of saturation bombing. Churchill refused to recommend him, however, and the choice fell on Fisher.

The national church plodded on in a reassuringly conservative way – particularly in the dreary dispensation of post-war England where the peace had been won but much else lost in every way. This raises another possible explanation. It is not surprising that the church sat tight, short of both money and men, sharing in the general austerity of the times and, under Fisher's somnolent ministrations, ill-equipped for anything tantamount to reform – internally or otherwise. A newly elected Labour Party was also addressing the inherent inequality of British society: the Beveridge Report, the Welfare State, the National Health Service and the genesis of secondary education represented genuine social achievements to which a depleted church could offer only benign assent and perhaps quiet gratitude that a renewed politics was being driven by high principles. Although incarnational theology and practice enjoyed less prominence during this period, important initiatives continued at the level of diocesan and parish life. Leslie Hunter and Ted Wickham made signal contributions that extended well beyond the normal confines of traditional church 'ambulance work'. Hunter's social concerns could be traced back to the aftermath of COPEC, and during the post-war years he cultivated imaginative and innovative links with industry.[57] Similarly, in retrospect, Wickham's book *Church and People in an Industrial City*[58] can be seen to have raised pressing questions in relation to the formation of an appropriate missionary structure in modern urban industrial communities.

Moving closer to our own time the writings of the former Anglican Bishop of Liverpool David Sheppard and the work of the Methodist theologian John Vincent reveal a sustained preoccupation with the concerns identified with the COPEC tradition. In his *Bias to the Poor*[59] Sheppard takes up the issues of poverty, housing and unemployment and justifies the intervention of the Church on these matters on the basis of the incarnation. Writing some years later of his rich and diverse ecumenical experience on Merseyside, typified by his close working relationship with the Roman Catholic Archbishop of Liverpool, Derek Worlock, he states:

> We believe that our Lord is present in our world in the enfleshed experience of people's lives . . . when we encounter

> deprived people, the incarnate Lord prompts us to ask why these persons are deprived . . . Can it seriously be contested that despair, loneliness, lack of vision and the crushing of the human spirit are also faith issues calling for the urgent attention of the Church?[60]

Such convictions led Sheppard and Worlock to act together for the sake of impoverished communities. In a joint letter to *The Times* (30 July 1980) they challenged the call by the Prime Minister Margaret Thatcher to unemployed young people to 'get mobile' and urged them instead, 'for God's sake stay'. In a leading article the following day, *The Daily Telegraph* castigated them as 'interventionist bishops'.

John Vincent has also been subjected to similar criticism. For many years, and particularly through the work of the Urban Theology Unit at Sheffield, he has been preoccupied with new forms of community living on the margins of Church and society. He looks to the Scriptures, in particular the Gospels, for guidance in matters of social and political action and writes powerfully (as we shall see later) of the value of acted parables and the prophetic witness of Christian groups. He has variously been accused of sullying religion in the murky waters of politics and for being naive in his use of the New Testament as the provider of solutions for contemporary social issues. If, as critics such as Ronald Preston have argued, there is no simple or easy way to move from the pastness and generalities of the Bible to the complexities of our present social order,[61] Vincent's work serves nevertheless as a living reminder that theological thought is inescapably political. It must always be concerned with who is doing what to whom, for good or ill, in our own rapidly changing times. Mindful of this truth and in a period of great social upheaval, the Church of England in the closing decades of the twentieth century produced a report on the inner cities that was to prove timely, controversial and far-reaching in its implications.

2 A Crisis in the Cities:

The Thatcher Years and the
Faith in the City Report

Not even the most prescient of social commentators could have foreseen the impact of *Faith in the City*[62] following its publication in 1985. In terms of practical outcomes it was without precedent in the chain of social thinking identified in the opening chapter, and from the outset readers were divided in their response. Critics saw it as evidence of the Church betraying its own membership by falling prey to Marxist theory.[63] Others praised its prophetic vision[64] and the astonishing levels of fund-raising it generated within the Church that led to thousands of community projects in the poorest towns and cities.[65] What made *Faith in the City* so special and why did it generate such controversy and excitement? To answer these questions we need to be aware of the provenance of the report and the momentous years leading to its publication.

In drawing attention to the persistence of urban poverty and inequality, *Faith in the City* contradicted the widespread assumption that poverty had been eliminated by post-1945 welfare reforms. Describing the plight of the areas covered by its research, the report confined itself to the marginalized and excluded who, if not actually starving, were deprived of what the rest of society regarded as the bare minimum for a decent life. In this respect, it constituted part of a considerable volume of research and literature that was concerned to keep the issue of poverty on the political agenda in the context of a relatively prosperous society. With regard to precedents, the revival of interest in the major aspects of social disadvantage and deprivation can be linked with the publication in 1965 of Abel-Smith and Townsend's *The Poor and the Poorest*.[66] This not only attracted much public attention but also brought poverty to prominence again as a major social issue.[67] Coincidentally it also led to the formation of the Child Poverty Action Group (CPAG) with the aim of educating public opinion on poverty issues.[68] *The Poor and the Poorest* represented a development of arguments to be found in earlier publications in the 1950s[69] (including Townsend's) which showed that, despite post-war social reforms, high taxation and low unemployment, there was poverty among the elderly, the unemployed and the sick. Added to this, as we have just seen, it also formulated the concept of relative poverty, an idea developed in Townsend's magisterial *Poverty in the United Kingdom*[70] that made an important and controversial contribution to the debate on social policy from 1979. Not everyone accepted the concept and sporadic attempts were made to deny its validity, usually by right-wing politicians or economists.[71] In the years that followed a substantial literature[72] was generated confined on the one hand to definitions and understandings of poverty and, on the other, to the more painstaking task of exploring from the inside the nature and dynamics of materially impoverished communities. One important example of the latter investigative approach, cited by *Faith in the City*,[73] is the work of Paul Harrison that shows how powerful and impersonal economic forces produce 'life under the cutting edge' for the poor in the inner city.[74] Confirmation of the rediscovery of urban poverty is also evident in other major publications. In 1977 the Government White Paper *Policy for the Inner Cities* conceded that a serious situation was developing in the major cities leading to decay and impoverishment. Four years later following riots in Toxteth and Brixton Lord Scarman drew attention to the complex pattern of conditions which lay at their root.[75]

Among these he recognized unemployment as a major factor[76] – a plausible assertion given that during the 1950s and 1960s unemployment had rarely exceeded half a million whereas throughout the 1980s it never dropped below 2.7 million. A year earlier Sir Douglas Black's report into inequalities in health care also established beyond reasonable doubt the links between social deprivation and ill health but his recommendations were never implemented because the Government conceded that they would be too expensive.[77]

On a wider front Britain was making a painful transition from an industrial to post-industrial economy – a change that witnessed a dramatic collapse in the textile, shipbuilding and mining industries. In addition there was the challenge of an increasingly competitive global economy that seemed beyond the control of national government. Hobsbawm comments:

> Nobody knew what to do about the vagaries of the world economy or possessed instruments to manage them. The major instrument for doing so in the Golden Age, government policy, nationally or internationally co-ordinated, no longer worked.[78]

In the world of politics, a seismic upheaval followed the election of the Conservative Government under Margaret Thatcher in May 1979. Influenced by the so-called 'New Right'[79] the Tory Government introduced a series of economic and political reforms which spurned the post-war political consensus and embraced the *laissez-faire* economics that typified the classical liberalism of the previous century. The intent to 'roll back the frontiers of the State' was given chilling expression in Mrs Thatcher's controversial comment that 'There is no such thing as society. There are individual men and women, and there are families.'[80] Financial markets now seemed to matter more than local communities and if the free hand of unfettered capitalism was making many rich it was equally excluding many from its privileges. Acquisitiveness and competition took precedence over notions of the common good and mutual care. In a critique of Mrs Thatcher's address to the General Assembly of the Church of Scotland in 1988, Jonathan Raban remarked:

> The jobless, and the poor on bottom-line wages, together with families whose procreative powers have outstripped their economic ones, are firmly excluded from the list of people to whom society owes sustenance, help and opportunity . . . The cynical view that she takes of her fellow citizens both rich and poor together with her polar methods for dealing with the laziness of the rich and the laziness of the poor are expressed with a fierce certainty and concision.[81]

An important part of the provenance of *Faith in the City* becomes intelligible when set against this background: on the one hand, a public policy with questionable moral foundations and, on the other, continuing urban unrest and deprivation in a prolonged period of structural economic change and relative economic decline. If we are to look for the more immediate sequence of events leading to the report, a case can be made for Archbishop Robert Runcie claiming some credit[82] for the initiative. In February 1982, the House of Lords debated the Scarman Report on the Brixton Riots. In welcoming the Report, Runcie spoke of the need for creative initiatives to foster the future of the inner city.[83] This represented his first public utterance on the subject but some nine months earlier Canon Eric James had written to *The Times*[84] concerning the relation of the Church of England to the inner-city areas. He urged the immediate appointment of an Archbishop's Commission and sent a copy to Runcie requesting a speedy reply to his suggestion. The Archbishop duly referred the matter to a group of urban bishops[85] and following a period of consultation and planning the commission was announced.[86] Runcie took no part in its work or conclusions: his contribution rested in the assembly of a highly talented team and his readiness to own what was plainly a serious and contentious document. He was aware of how easily it could misfire or be traduced but was equally determined not to be outwitted.[87] This coolness and caution, assisted by the promptings of Eric James, made possible a distinctive and creative response that led in turn to a national debate on the state and future of the cities.

To open the pages of *Faith in the City* again, even after a passage of almost 20 years, is to be struck immediately by its sense of urgency and the range of its concerns. In relation to matters of public policy, its recommendations cover a broad range of issues resulting from the commission's travels and enquiries. Employment and housing figure prominently followed by urban policy, health, social care and community work, education and young people, order and law. It is important to remember that it was not a textbook written for a restricted readership but a call to action, an appeal based on a reasoned argument inviting a response. The commission saw a nation confronted by a *grave and fundamental injustice* in the cities, yet despite the continuing deterioration no adequate response was being made to this alarming situation by government, Church or nation.[88] Despite its anxious tone, the report carefully delineates, on the basis of its research, the wider implications of this social injustice. Its pages recognize that:

- the effects of social and economic problems on the vulnerable are not restricted to material deprivation, but also cut them off from the mainstream of national life and diminish them
- problems of poverty, unemployment and other social ills are features of the injustice and inequality rooted in the structure of society and traceable through every institution, including the Church
- Christians must be ready to ask if there is any serious political will to enable the poor to have a proper stake in the life of the nation.[89]

At no point does the report suggest that the challenge of the cities is the responsibility of Government alone. It calls the Church to put its own house in order for the purpose of co-operating with other agencies and institutions for the common good. In particular, urban churches should become local, outward-looking and participating with a clear ecumenical bias.[90] There are proposals for laity development, increased levels of giving, new patterns of ministry and worship, the proper use of Church buildings to serve more effectively in areas of need and the setting up of a new Church Urban Fund. Racism is also acknowledged and a new commission on black Anglicans is advocated to respond to the alienation experienced by many black people in relation to the Church of England.[91] Addressing its General Synod in February 1986, the Archbishop of Canterbury commented:

> This report makes pressing claims on our Church's mind and heart and will. We begin to grasp that if the Church is to be truly a sign of the kingdom and love of God present in our midst, the longer-term implications of the changes required will be more radical and more painful than have yet been spelt out.[92]

These demands emerged not only from the findings of the commission but also from the theological assumptions that informed its social analysis and policy proposals. In calling to mind the scriptural mandate to 'remember the poor' (Gal. 2.10) its members were insistent that this duty had to go beyond acts of individual charity or service and take the form of social and political action that sought to alter situations that cause poverty and distress. Such action could be linked to a long Christian tradition of social justice reaching back to the Old Testament prophets and entailed in Jesus' proclamation of the kingdom of God. In an almost identical vein to the writings of Maurice more than a century earlier the report makes a plea for collective action and solidarity one with another as counter-measures to the rampant individualism of public and private life.[93] A few paragraphs later the report does not flinch from acknowledging that the common good and compassion alike are being adversely affected by government policies:

> Christians should be particularly sensitive to trends or policies which . . . can be shown to be making the plight of some classes of citizens actually worse, and if moreover the resources available to those who seek to alleviate this plight are being reduced, it is a clear duty for the Church to sound a warning that our society may be losing the 'compassionate' character which is still desired by the majority of its members.[94]

For the commission, a compassionate society is bound up with the theological concept of koinonia or community. Drawing on the Pauline emphasis on building up the Christian body, the report's doctrine of humanity is one that points to mutuality, solidarity and interdependence as the means whereby the Christian community is responsive to the whole of society and the God-given potential of each person is developed.[95] What made *Faith in the City* so exciting on first reading was its conviction that this vision of human flourishing and community was still to be found within the concrete (and sometimes harsh) experience of urban life:

> We believe that God, though infinitely transcendent, is also to be found, despite all appearances, in the apparent waste lands of our inner cities and housing estates . . . that the city is not to be shunned as a concentration of evil but enjoyed as a unique opportunity for human community.[96]

These affirmations of the urban were 'felt on the pulse' by the commission. As members travelled the country taking evidence, they had each been challenged to think and act differently and to stand more closely alongside the poor and powerless.[97] There can be little doubt such experiences contributed to the integrity and impact of the report upon its wide readership.[98] Lord Scarman commented:

> Whether or not one agrees with its proposals, or with all or any of them, it is the finest face to face analysis and description of the problems of the inner city and of the other urban priority areas where those problems exist that we have yet seen. In the long run, it will take its place, I believe, as a classic description of one of the most serious troubles in British society.[99]

The praise was just: the commission had listened carefully to people to an extent that was untypical of either church or government agencies.[100] That its members were able to speak with subversive authority owed much to the experiences that had shaped their convictions and informed their public statements and recommendations.

In the initial furore following the publication of the report, critics ignored or overlooked the fact that most of its main recommendations – 38 out of a total of 61 were addressed to the Church of England itself. So how did this venerable institution respond to a wide-ranging set of proposals that challenged local urban churches in particular to reimagine their role? At one level there was substantial evidence of fresh alliances that had enlivened local communities.[101] From personal experience as Chair of the Hull Faith in the City Group, I recall a community lunch with the Archbishop of York as the guest speaker. It proved an impressive ecumenical occasion with representatives drawn from local churches and the city. The Archbishop took as his theme 'A Matter of Hope: Redeeming the City'. The example is important not simply because it arises from personal experience but rather that it demonstrated how the 'Call for Action' of *Faith in the City* was interpreted so variously and often with a strong bias towards pastoral care, ecumenism and partnerships in the community. In Bradford the Faith in the City Forum embraced representatives of nine Christian denominations and became a significant agent in local urban renewal.[102]

With regard to the increasingly important issue of racist attitudes within the Church and community, *Faith in the City* has contributed to the setting up of the Committee on Black Anglican Concerns (CBAC), which assists dioceses in developing programmes and strategies for combating racism. In 1991 the Diocese of Oxford published *The Seeds of Hope Report*, duly debated by General Synod in the same year. A study pack has subsequently been published for parishes wanting to explore the issue of racism and justice.[103] A major initiative in 1994 brought together, for the first time in the Church of England, people from parishes (black and white) with bishops and key advisers for a weekend residential conference to celebrate the diversity of gifts that black Anglicans bring to their congregations and communities. Racial Justice Sunday is now observed annually across the denominations and, as recent disturbances in Burnley and Oldham have demonstrated (where racial and religious affiliations were among the factors), the long journey towards racial equality will need to remain a significant item on the churches' agendas.

In terms of fundraising, the Church Urban Fund (CUF) can be linked directly to the earlier Mission Alongside the Poor initiative of the Methodist Church. Both made possible an imaginative range of projects relating to poverty, unemployment and social care and enhanced significantly the churches' role as they shared the hardships of their communities. That they were prepared to stay and serve was a source of great encouragement to others. The following extract from a paper by Don May, a Methodist minister, and Margaret Simey, a Liverpool City Councillor, is one of many testimonies that could be cited. Here Margaret Simey, a non-church member, describes why this presence mattered:

> In effect, the churches stood for an alternative way of life to that of the individualism and materialism which threatened our survival as a human society. Their efforts were often as futile as our own but I am convinced that merely to exist amongst us on those terms was a positive contribution. I

know that I personally found that my own sense of commitment to what I call socialism and they call Christianity
was refreshed by even the most casual contact at some committee meeting or youth club. Those whose values are put to
the test of extreme and continuing stress learn by harsh
experience that no man can live wholly unto himself, but
the struggle to keep alive any sense of social duty is often a
desperate one. The mere existence in our midst of a handful
of people who were there for no other reason than to keep
that flag flying I believe to have been a greater importance
than we, or perhaps they realised. There was an unspoken
comfort to be derived from the fact that someone still had
faith in the ideal of the caring community even though bitter
disillusion had eroded our own conviction.[104]

Much of the commendable work at the local level was
pastoral in nature, concerned for individuals and communities
in need but, certainly from an Anglican perspective, less
inclined to address the deep-seated issues of powerlessness
and political marginalization raised by *Faith in the City*.
Alleviating the symptoms of urban decay proved for most
local churches a more manageable and less contentious task
than tackling the wider causes of poverty and inequality. This
reluctance was not altogether surprising and, arguably,
reflected a deeply ingrained and cautious Anglican instinct
that has over generations preferred a theology of good works
to a theology of transformation as the appropriate expression
of true religion. A theology of the kingdom with its challenge
to institutions as well as individuals has proved less palatable
– partly out of human disinclination to face its disturbing
social implications and then again as a consequence of belonging to a national church that at the local level still regards
civility, stability and compassion as epitomizing English
Christianity. The Anglican character seems naturally disposed
to works of charity: embracing the ambiguities of social and
political activism, however, is a discipline that has still to be
mastered (perhaps even acknowledged) by many Christians,

despite the summons of *Faith in the City* and the tradition of incarnational theology which both defined and preceded it.[105] In fairness the commission recognized this danger from the outset, noting that whereas many Church of England members were ready to help victims of misfortune, fewer were willing to rectify injustices in society.[106]

It is worth recalling at this point that the promotion of Christian witness in the inner cities was clearly not meant to be the only initiative by which the success (or otherwise) of *Faith in the City* would be judged. The commission devoted much more space to questions of public policy resulting from its enquiry and was clear that the regeneration of the inner cities would only be achieved through a major increase in government spending and private-sector investment. It set out in some detail how these aims could be achieved.

As to the outcomes of these proposals, at one level the report exercised considerable influence on British political debate. Following her election victory in 1987, Mrs Thatcher acknowledged that 'we've got a big job to do in some of those inner cities'.[107] Elsewhere, local authorities debated its findings and recommendations and sent delegates to conferences on *Faith in the City* organized by the dioceses. An Inner Cities Religious Council (ICRC) was also set up to promote better ways of working together in inner cities and housing estates. The Revd David Horn, former Secretary to the ICRC, recognized 'a causal link between *Faith in the City* and the emergence of the ICRC. The latter could not have happened without the former.'[108] The extent to which the council promoted new ways of Christian denominations representing community interests is evident from the following Methodist perspective:

> This is a new experience for all of us. Some of us are more used to interfaith dialogue with its long and painful growth in trust and friendship followed by specific social action in local communities. Here we are beginning rather than ending with the consequences, and picking up each other's various ways of thinking through and implementing faith as

we go along. Our ways of looking at things are as diverse as our beliefs. Some think of the whole nation and its needs, others stress the morality of their particular tradition, some have particular regard for equality and well-being of the minority group they represent and some of us have more direct experience of the inner city than others. We are growing in understanding and all the time learning from each other.[109]

If these varied initiatives represented real political gains, there was also disquieting evidence which showed that an actual shift in Government policy towards urban issues was much less marked and many of the commission's central recommendations were rejected or ignored. It can be seen now that the respective urban agendas of Church and Government were fundamentally incompatible. The commission had failed to appreciate the shift in ideology under the Thatcher administration and the extent to which a Prime Minister wedded to notions of competition and rugged individualism would brook no alternative on social and economic policy.[110]

All this took place in the 1980s. Not so very long ago, yet the scale and pace of change in the intervening years and the ways in which cities continue to evolve in response to factors ranging from the local to the international have led some commentators to view *Faith in the City* as part of our past – not yet antiquated but superseded by later events.[111] As will be shown in Part Two, the emerging urban order is assuming new and volatile configurations and local churches often appear as vulnerable and marginalized as the poor they serve. But does this mean that the report should now be regarded as history, important history admittedly, but nothing more? Its obituary notices seem premature set against the imaginative projects it continues to generate through the CUF and the contribution that it is still able to make to the debate concerning the connection between faith and urban communities. In a recent letter to the religious press, the Chairman of the Urban Bishops' Panel wrote:

The significance of the Report was seen very clearly in the 1998 Lambeth Conference, and was the inspiration of the resolution calling for a 'Faith in an Urban World' commission. In recent conversations, both with government ministers and city councillors, we have found, as urban bishops, that there are constant references to *Faith in the City* – and this is 15 years after its publication.[112]

The one thing lacking in the letter is a crucial caveat provided by the Methodist Church in its publication, *The Cities*.[113] Theologically and pastorally, it is axiomatic that urban mission should remain committed to the poor and disadvantaged in keeping with the spirit of the report and the precepts of Scripture. But the challenge now is how to defend and articulate the belief that urban contexts frequently characterized by marginalization and social fragmentation are still good places to live and may even mediate the presence of God. Furthermore, where are the resources to be found (beyond the immediate provision of funding) that will enable local church leaders and congregations to stay in the city and engage in the re-creation of community in the global context of a new millennium?

It is in these vital areas – the need to provide, on the one hand, a more comprehensive understanding of how cities are produced and the largely autonomous forces working on them and, on the other, the means of building strength and a deeper sense of identity at the local level – that the limitations of *Faith in the City* become evident.

Despite its title, the report confines itself to Urban Priority Areas (UPAs), to their pain and poverty and the remedial measures deemed necessary. They are defined as locations on maps with z scores that point to multiple deprivation calling for specific programmes of regeneration or the concerted action of local agencies. But the city in its wider aspects is about power, self-assertion and diverse activities; it represents at any time both a statement concerning the limitations and possibilities of human beings and also a volatile conduit for the economic forces that enhance or diminish the inner city. Noting the emphasis of the commission on UPAs, Haddon Willmer comments:

> There is a danger that the impression is created that the problem of the Urban Priority Areas can be discerned and tackled in detachment from the dynamics of the whole society with its economics and politics provided . . . enough resources are devoted to them. The truth lies in the other direction. The existence of Urban Priority Areas reveals something about the working of the whole economic, political and moral system in which we all live. Urban Priority Areas demand direct and immediate action; they also drive inquiry back to the city.[114]

The point is well made. UPAs need to be understood in the political/economic context that is 'the city' rather than just a discrete element within it. *Faith in the City* does honour its remit to bring the needs of the inner cities to the attention of the nation and its broadly incarnational ecclesiology reveals the insidious and structural elements that produce marginalized communities. What it failed to do, however, was embrace the globalization of economic life and engage with the diverse and unpredictable processes that create the modern city. This is a new and intellectually demanding requirement of urban mission that has any claim to relevance in the public realm. Among other things it calls for the dimension of a public theology – a task that will be taken up in Chapter 5.

Another conspicuous omission is the absence of any serious attention given by the report to the traditional disciplines of prayer, spirituality and the use of Scripture. Without these and in particular in the testing context of the UPAs,[115] even the best-intentioned activities quickly become indistinguishable from purely secular initiatives and may fall prey to apathy and indifference. Yet the report devotes just four pages to worship and confines itself to liturgical utility – the organizing of services, the importance of language and the place of children in the Church.[116] Little is said overtly concerning prayer, meditation and silence or the ways in which a disciplined urban spirituality might be fostered through a careful attention to the Bible. It seems that the commission simply assumed that local congregations would recognize the need for both prayer and spirituality if mission was to advance in the UPAs.[117] The paucity of specifically scriptural material is still surprising, however, particularly in view of the fact that the commission's internal theologian, Anthony Harvey, was a biblical scholar. The situation is different now and it is encouraging to note the current renewal of interest in Scripture and the resonances between the fragile urban communities of the New Testament and the practical discipleship of local inner-city congregations today.[118] In Part Three I shall argue that the Bible along with prayer and worship are particular gifts that the Church can offer to the city that also nurture Christian distinctiveness and confidence.

Our historical excursion ends here. Despite evidence of limitations and failures the journey has also shown how churches have made creative and sometimes incisive contributions to the economic and social fortunes of the city. The history of urban mission for the better part of the last two centuries provides grounds for hope and a recognizable tradition of Christian care and compassion.[119] But we have also been alerted to the necessity of making sense of the emerging urban order and the complex phenomenon of increasing globalization. Both require fresh thinking and new patterns of engagement. The next chapter addresses the first requirement – how we are to understand this dynamic context so that we might begin to think about it theologically.

Part Two

The Emerging Urban Order

3 Cities Today:
Local and Global

The contemporary urban landscape invites awe and apprehension in equal measure. So much has changed since the Archbishop's Commission criss-crossed the nation from 1983 to 1984 in search of evidence and much, depressingly, remains the same. More people than ever before[120] are living in urban areas characterized by diversity, competition and commonalities:

> Urban places have many similarities of physical appearance, economic structure and social organization and are beset by the same problems of employment, housing, transport and environmental quality.[121]

Facing up to these issues has been increasingly hampered by social disintegration and the extent to which consumerism and technology tend to vitiate the notions of mutual support and co-operation that inform the ideal of the city as a place where civil aspirations are acknowledged and realized.[122] In this respect there is some justification in the claim that *Faith in the City* was caught between what Michael Serres has described as the Old City and the New City.[123] Although the commission recognized that a serious situation was developing in the Urban Priority Areas (UPAs), the more perceptive critics of its report have argued that its endorsement of human solidarity, collaboration and community failed to grasp the extent to which such values were being jeopardized by rapid change in the cities. Ward comments:

It never asked whether the social atomism of city-life had moved beyond being able to collaborate; it never asked who contributed and why, and who couldn't or wouldn't contribute; it never asked about the growing numbers who have already opted out – who have already opted for a virtual reality (in drugs, in drink, in interactive computer games, in play-station fantasies, in film, in televiewing) . . . It referred continually to the concept of nation (and implicitly to a nationalism) that flew in the face of increasing globalization.[124]

How far modern cities have actually turned into what Ward describes as 'radically eclectic places where each pursues his or her own consumer interests under the ever watchful eye of surveillance cameras'[125] will be considered later in this chapter. For now it is necessary only to acknowledge that in important respects it is the case that 'we have not passed this way heretofore'.[126] The emerging realities of urban life today need to be examined against the background of a new global economy and the disparate needs, interests and expectations that define urban life and work. This necessity is twofold. First, any mission strategy hoping to exert a positive influence on this shifting and dynamic context will need to reflect theologically on the public events that form 'part of the texture of our lives'.[127] This conviction has underpinned much of the social thought and practice identified in the previous chapters. Second, this painstaking task of interpretation may be seen as a faithful response to the scriptural mandate to read the signs of the times.[128] The profound implications of this gospel teaching and the corollary that Christians should live, learn and serve within the particularities of the present rather than any other times are set down incisively by Ward:

Time is the unfolding of God's grace . . . Those involved with the living out of those faiths stand consciously enfolded in that unfolding . . . within *this* time, rather than *that,* in *this* space rather than *that* space, moving and moved in *this* direction rather than *that* direction . . . And so Christians must constantly ask 'What time is this in which we stand?' For this question is inseparable from 'What am I called to be and do?' And 'What is the will of God?' . . . To ask what time it is is to begin to rewrite the teaching of the faith (and begin a teaching of the faith) for the contemporary cultural context; to reinscribe the cultural context within the Christian faith and so bear the Christian tradition into the future.[129]

Ascertaining the time and the specific theological response demanded by it raises three issues. First, how have the cities fared since 1985, particularly in response to the plethora of government initiatives and property-led regeneration schemes? Second, reference will need to be made to the impact of globalization and how new technologies and the free play of market economies are shaping the emerging urban order. Third, the potential of the modern city to remain a centre for human conviviality and flourishing needs to be addressed in relation to the claim that contemporary urban life is primarily characterized by fragmentation and a disregard for all those who lack the skill, talent or energy to share in its achievements and celebrations.[130]

As *Faith in the City* made a strong case for government intervention at the level of urban regeneration, we need to ask how the cities have changed in the years since 1985 under the impact of State-directed policies. In seeking to answer the question a paradox quickly emerges: during the period under review a great deal of time and huge budgets have been directed towards the cities. City Challenge in the early 1990s has been followed by the Single Regeneration Budget (SRB) in 1994 and, since the election of the Labour Administration in 1997, a veritable blizzard of schemes, all with the ostensible aim of improving the urban landscape.[131] Two major Government reports have also been published that specifically address the issue of urban regeneration and the current state of the towns and cities. Following the report of the Social Exclusion Unit on deprived neighbourhoods[132] a consultation document[133] has set out a national strategy for neighbourhood renewal:

> This report sets out a framework for the National Strategy, seeking feedback from everyone with an interest in deprived neighbourhoods, as input to the Government's plans and – crucially – to its spending decisions for the next three years. It sets out analysis, ideas and key questions for discussion, and asks other partners to help improve these ideas and think what they could contribute. The aim of the Strategy is to arrest the wholesale decline of deprived neighbourhoods, to reverse it, and to prevent it from recurring. Success should be measured against a simple goal – to narrow the gap between deprived areas and the rest of the country by dramatically improving outcomes – with more jobs, better educational attainment, less crime and better health – in the most deprived areas.[134]

An Urban White Paper,[135] the first for 20 years, has also been issued, incorporating a raft of measures that indicate a long-term commitment to action in the cities in the belief that they 'not only concentrate problems . . . but also solutions. They hold the key to our common future.'[136] The report goes on to acknowledge the ambitious nature of this projected programme and the extent to which an urban renaissance will require co-operation at every level:

> The Government through the Urban Policy Unit will be working closely with towns and cities in taking forward the principles in this White Paper. This is an ambitious long-term programme of change and development in our towns and cities. If places are for people then people must help make the places. The Government has set out its commitment. It will lead the way forward but action will ultimately depend on everyone contributing to change whether as individuals in their own street and neighbourhood, as investors and businesses in shaping the economy of their city, or as local representatives creating the vision for the city.[137]

This profusion of programmes and proposals suggests that there has patently been no shortage of urban initiatives or good intentions on the part of the Government. When John Prescott declared that the 'aim is to reduce or eliminate the gap between prosperous and disadvantaged communities'[138] this could be seen as a serious and principled endeavour to break the cycle of economic and social problems that entrench deprivation. There is also, however, the concomitant danger of too many programmes operating simultaneously leading to communities drowning in a sea of initiatives and agencies lacking the essential co-ordination that makes for effective strategies.[139] Furthermore a commendable concern for the socially and economically marginalized still begs the question of how urban regeneration policies can be effectively married to the aims of the Social Exclusion Unit. For example, can a regional development authority that is mandated to promote economic competitiveness and attract investment, simultaneously focus on the needs of the most deprived communities? Prior to the election of Labour in 1997 a publication sponsored by the Department of the Environment commented:

> The likely future based on current trends is, if anything, one of increasingly marked inner-city problems, increasing spatial concentration of disadvantage in inner-city areas and outer estates, and increasing polarisation and lack of social and economic cohesion between inner cities and other areas.[140]

Although the Urban White Paper and the *National Strategies for Neighbourhood Renewal* clearly aim to avoid this grim prospect, questions remain to the effect that in this particular instance insufficient thought has been given to long-term economic implications with their tendency to promote marginalization and these may be only indicative of a well-meaning administration acting too hastily in order to be seen to be doing things.[141]

Despite evidence of Government largesse towards the cities there is therefore, as yet, no convincing evidence to demonstrate that the money and effort directed towards urban renewal in recent years have significantly improved the most deprived areas. Statistical data actually show that inequality, relative poverty, poor health and limited opportunities remain discernible features of urban life.[142] These sobering facts are also confirmed by recent surveys. Two examples will suffice. Over a period of more than a year, members of a Council of Churches for Britain and Northern Ireland Working Party visited many urban areas.[143] Experiences and reactions were depressingly similar to those of the Archbishop's Commission in 1983:

> We have returned shocked and saddened by the sharpness of contrast we have found everywhere between a favoured majority on the one hand and those on the other who are left out . . . Wherever we went we saw increasing riches and increasing poverty side by side.[144]

In matters of health inequalities in deprived areas, recent work undertaken by The King's Fund has also generated an important debate with clear implications for urban policy makers. Writing in his Foreword, Sir Donald Acheson, formerly the Government's Chief Medical Officer for England comments:

> The wide and increasing social differential in premature illness and death in Britain should be a matter for serious public concern. In 1995 it seems almost commonplace to repeat what has been known for at least twenty years . . . namely that in this country death rates at most ages (including childhood) are two or three times as high in lower as in upper social classes and among the least well-off this leads to an attenuation of life of at least eight years together with a corresponding increased burden of ill health and disability. Today the question is not whether these facts are valid but who cares and what can be done about them. In the

circumstances it is particularly unfortunate that the issue has become a party political football . . . We now see that any successful effort to reduce inequalities in health must be based on a broad range of actions involving almost every aspect of society. The approach to a number of the policies which must be considered, such as the redistribution of income, the creation of jobs, investment in new and improved housing (here the report argues that the funding problem is not as problematical as is often thought) and the health impact assessment, is controversial across the political parties.[145]

This lack of conspicuous success in eradicating social disadvantage and inequalities is not wholly explained by the lack of co-ordination or undue haste described earlier. Critics of Government initiatives have not been slow to point out that a legitimate enthusiasm for the renewal of the material fabric of the cities must also be accompanied by a readiness to address the social conditions that exacerbate decline. The following extract is contained in a memorandum from the Anglican Urban Bishops' Panel in response to the final report of the Government's Urban Task Force:[146]

The report says little about multi-cultural identity, social exclusion and racism . . . is it possible to reshape and repopulate our urban areas solely by the imposition of enlightened planning, management and environmental measures? Local consultation had been given hardly a passing nod and the cost of regeneration to the individual and community is barely conceded.[147]

Similarly, in a submission to the Social Exclusion Unit, Stephen Hill, a Director of Capital Action (specializing in regeneration projects) commented that 'initiatives have failed to eradicate poverty and inequality because policies have been directed at the treatment of symptoms rather than causes'[148] identified with class, race, housing and unemployment. Paul

Hackwood and Phil Shiner have also been critical of property-led regeneration schemes that leave local people more deprived and divided than before.[149]

The above criticisms suggest that big budgets and good intentions alone are not enough to deliver an urban renaissance. The point is conceded in the White Paper *Our Towns and Cities*, but at this relatively early stage it is impossible to judge to what extent its rhetorical insistence that urban policies entail more than bricks and mortar[150] will be translated into strategies that enable local communities to shape their future while simultaneously addressing the endemic problems that exacerbate exclusion, poverty and decline. There will certainly need to be a greater degree of sophistication and strategic awareness in Government-led interventions so that disparate programmes are more effectively co-ordinated and policy makers are clearer as to whether urban problems should be understood as 'problems fundamentally *of* cities or problems *in* cities'.[151] The distinction is important as David Sheppard has noted: 'It is predictable, inevitable perhaps that some urban communities will forever be seen as places to get out of rather than places in which people move in and out of.'[152]

Endorsing this point, it can be argued that much greater recognition needs to be given to the fact that urban unease or fragmentation cannot simply be understood in terms of problems that are concentrated in particular areas. The urban as a whole system needs more careful interrogation so that cross-departmental initiatives proceed from the basic understanding that the quality of urban life, in terms of material dereliction and renewal, is intimately linked to the issues raised by the Urban Bishops' Panel, including racism, social exclusion, health and unemployment. If any government fails to acknowledge this crucial link, the chances of a cohesive, functional and convivial urban future remain in jeopardy.

This brief survey indicates that the millennium city continues to raise formidable issues for the churches and not just in terms of the perennial problems of social need and deprivation. Rather they have to do with the fact that, increasingly, the emerging urban order is a problematic location that, on the one hand, appears unresponsive to unco-ordinated interventionist projects and, on the other, can easily threaten any sense of the city as a collective good through the complex interplay of economic and social factors that impinge upon each other. Unanticipated challenges and the increasingly global culture of the urban call for new patterns of discernment and the recognition that the city can no longer be thought of 'as having one geography and history (and therefore one future)'.[153] The recent Urban White Paper notes:

> Our economy has changed radically with the role of manufacturing declining and the growth of service, new technology and creative industries. We need to compete on a global scale for jobs and investment. The challenge of protecting our environment locally and globally becomes ever more urgent. We are a densely populated country in which people are continuing to leave our major conurbations with major implications for urban areas . . . and rural communities.[154]

If complexity defines the city, it is also the case that it is evolving in different ways. Its end is by definition unknown for, as we shall now see, it is being shaped by contingencies that can elude constraints or controls, for example, the interplay of economic forces that are neither wholly localized nor fully regulated. These constitute part of its energy and fascination but also determine, in some measure, its status as victim, beneficiary or survivor.[155] As globalization is increasingly seen to occupy a pivotal place in any comprehensive reading of the contemporary city, we can now look at its effect on urban life in a little more detail.

A generation ago, the slogan of one of our Sunday newspapers boasted that within its pages 'all human life was there'. The same can now be said of our modern towns and cities. To walk down any street is not simply to encounter different ethnic communities but to witness the remarkable interplay between the local and the global:

> You will see goods displayed that have been made in the factories and sweatshops of the South; fruit and vegetables, some of which have travelled by air; financial institutions carrying the names of distant states; and meeting-places labelled in numerous languages. Magazines and newspapers will combine the issues of communities thousands of miles away and those in the immediate locality. Posters and graffiti will advocate the political causes of regions on other continents. The experience of such a street scene can no longer be considered exotic: it is becoming the reality in numerous small provincial towns and cities, as well as those places previously thought of as cosmopolitan cities. The diverse ethnic cultures encountered will form part of the civic community – sending children to its schools, participating in local politics, paying local and national taxes, and calling on local medical and social services, just as numerous groups of immigrants have done before them.[156]

Globalization is now the preferred term to describe the *interconnectedness* of the world. In May 1997 the International Monetary Fund (IMF) provided the following definition in its twice-yearly World Economic Outlook:

> Globalization refers to the growing interdependencies of countries worldwide through the increasing volume and variety of cross-border transactions in goods and services, and of international capital flows; and also through the rapid and widespread diffusion of all kinds of technology.[157]

In one sense the concept is not new. International trading goes back centuries with the Industrial Revolution providing a powerful impetus in the creation of a single international economy. The words of Prince Albert as he opened the Great Exhibition in 1851 are almost eerily contemporary:

We are living at a period of most wonderful transition which tends rapidly to accomplish that great end to which indeed all history points – the realization of the unity of mankind . . . The distances which separated the different nations and parts of the globe are rapidly vanishing before the achievements of modern invention, and we can traverse them with incredible ease . . . Thought is communicated with the rapidity, and even by the power, of lightning . . . The products of all quarters of the globe are placed at our disposal, and we have only to choose which is the best and cheapest for our purposes, and the powers of production are entrusted to the stimulus of competition and capitalism.[158]

As the distances between the nations diminished, the bulk of the world's most important business was also conducted in what the urban commentator Patrick Geddes described in 1915 as 'world cities'. They are easily identifiable today: London, New York and Tokyo represent a snapshot of the major economic powers of the past 150 years and remain the centres of the international economy and world trade. In 1991 Saskia Sassen coined the term 'global cities' to represent these locations where the 'wealth of nations' is measured, made and exchanged.

What has changed a century and a half on from Prince Albert's opening speech – and it is a transition that now makes Victorian society seem like another world – is the extent, scale and speed of change itself. The power of instantaneous global communication, the growth of multinational corporations, the development of migratory labour forces and the deregulation of financial markets – all of these constitute new social and economic phenomena with profound implications for our *interconnectedness*.

Electronic banking and the Internet abolish distance and provide us with access to goods and amenities regardless of location in a matter of seconds. Former President Bill Clinton noted on leaving office that when he entered the White House in 1993 there were just 50 registered websites. In the year 2000 there were more than 350 million. Big business generates revenues in excess of the gross domestic product of individual nations and an oil company can register profit margins at the rate of £300 per second.[159] Investments are geared to locations that are likely to yield the highest competitive advantage at minimum cost. Nike shoes provides an interesting case study: 6,000 people in Oregon are engaged in advertising, research and development. Production in recent years, however, has shifted from South Korea to Thailand and Indonesia.[160]

This ability to shift production from place to place means that jobs – particularly in the manufacturing industries – have become more vulnerable. In some cases it signifies that large-scale manufacturing has left British cities and will not return except in a compact high-tech form. Burgeoning information and service industries[161] can help to mitigate the impact of this transition but cities still face the challenge of finding new sources of investment and employment as capital flows freely between countries and consumer choice drives economic trends. A poignant evocation of how a once thriving location can be left behind in this heady but unstable economic environment is provided in the two juxtaposed views of Sheffield which open the film *The Full Monty*. Ward comments:

> The first view of the city, which unfolds as the credits and titles roll, takes the form of a promotional exercise on behalf of the city in the 1960s. The newsreel effect creates the sense of a documentary. And what is being documented is Sheffield, the home of steel manufacture, as a city of industrial and commercial plenty. The second view, which follows the credits, is an interior shot of one of the steel sheds in the 1990s, now abandoned, gutted, derelict. The camera looks down impassively on the scene from the ceiling and into the corner of the frame walk two of the former workers-turned-petty-thieves bearing an old girder (symbol of that erstwhile plenty).[162]

These opening shots convey more powerfully than any economic treatise a singular truth: the flows and processes of a global economy are transactional not moral, concerned primarily with financial outcomes not values and able, equally, to generate winners and losers in their train. In short, globalization is about new configurations of power: 'some people are more in charge of it than others . . . some are more on the receiving end of it than others; some are effectively imprisoned by it'.[163]

One of the more encouraging features of Christian witness in recent years has come through the overt resistance to a system that has scant regard for consequences and exists alongside widespread human suffering. Billions of financial transactions, investments and acquisitions are driven by the demand for profits rather than social justice and world economic policies barely touch the 1.2 billion people who exist on less than a dollar a day.[164] The Jubilee 2000 campaign, led by Christian Aid as the major ecumenical relief agency, raised a new awareness across the churches, concerning how the world works and achieved some success in its aim of reducing the Third World debt. Christian Aid also collaborated with Church Action on Poverty and their joint report emphasized the need to 'bring moral arguments to the globalization, exclusion and poverty debates'.[165] More recently the Catholic Bishops' Conference of England and Wales has issued a powerful statement, 'Trade and Solidarity' (1 June 2003), that examines the economics of trade, particularly its impact on developing countries and as a key element in international economic justice. There is a growing recognition of the enormity and power of global economics and simultaneously a challenge to resist or even subvert the 'placeless logic'[166] of international capital. This concern extends beyond the Christian community. In December 1997, Manchester's Christmas celebrations were sponsored by the car manufacturers Renault. The generous donor, in a surfeit of seasonal spirit, had attached its own logo to the municipal Christmas tree. In the dead of night a person or persons unknown climbed the tree, removed the Renault diamond and replaced it with a gold star.[167]

We can either be amused or alarmed by this anecdote. It can be viewed as a touch of Gallic insouciance that is in turn countermanded by an equally resolute act of local defiance. Or is it an insidious instance of transnational corporate arrogance that is emblematic of the struggle between people and corporations that will be a recurring battle in the twenty-first century?[168] At the very least it raises important questions about the power of business corporations, the challenge they represent to independent national policies and their impact on our towns and cities. With the demise of local manufacturing, it is possible to conjecture the emergence of a new urban social class structure: the skilled blue-collar class shrinks; the unskilled class is consigned to low-paid unstable work and a new service class emerges providing a range of amenities and support services demanded by the affluent. Much contemporary writing depicts the post-millennium city of extremes dividing the rich from the poor[169] with the imaginative or fortunate deserting at the earliest opportunity:

> The areas of east Manchester, London and Leeds have lost more than 80% of their population during the twentieth-century . . . This growing exodus from our cities is covering our countryside with a suburban sprawl that is the lowest density in Europe.[170]

The limitation of this rather bleak view of urban life is that it fails to recognize or acknowledge that cities have more complex socio-economic structures than the model indicates. There is fragmentation and invidious degrees of social differentiation but not to the extent that speaks exclusively of bipolarization. To accept, for example, the facts of homelessness, unemployment and derelict areas also requires the recognition that the scale, extent and obduracy of these problems are shaped by the specific histories, traditions of urban planning and, crucially, the commitment of politicians, community workers, churches and interest groups that is capable of fostering quite different urban forms and processes.[171] The dualistic model therefore is needlessly skewed in the way it interprets the flow and impact of economic forces. Cities are not condemned to be merely passive receptors: some may capitulate but others do not. In particular instances, the shape of a city is determined, in part, by what governments, local citizens, activists and bureaucrats deem to be important. To give a recent European example: Premier Michel Rocard imposed a regulation that every square metre of office space built in Paris had to be offset by two square metres of housing.[172] With a measure of vigilance and imagination, crude market forces can be resisted and a city can become a more discreet focus which asserts that the making of community is as important as the making of money. Economic determinism alone does not shape the urban agenda. And even the policies of the international entrepreneur are occasionally shaped by ethical/long-term business considerations that are neither predatory nor entirely self-serving. Following the decision of Toyota to make more cars in Britain the company President Hiroshi Okuda stated: 'Our commitment to the UK and European operations is a long-term commitment that is not affected by short-term fluctuations in demand and sales, or other economic factors.'[173] There is space therefore at the local level for creativity, innovation and, where necessary, resistance whilst recognizing simultaneously that the impact of globalization on the cities will continue to be marked:

> Globalization and economic growth, driven by the relentless engine of technological advance, 'cannot be wished away'. Nor can their complex nature, or tendency to generate winners and losers. From the late eighteenth century, gathering pace ever since, the trend has been to greater productivity, to produce more with less. Under 3% are now engaged in agriculture in Britain and the United States, growing more than ever before. So it will be with manufacturing, and then services. And so it is happening. Such

technological advances as biotechnology and robotics will drive these tendencies further and further, aided and abetted by globalization processes and information and communication technologies.[174]

Apart from the examples just provided, is there more evidence to demonstrate what can be achieved locally in relation to the competitive struggle of the world market? A good example of urban regeneration in a time of economic uncertainty and rapid change has been provided recently by the city of Salford. Although it lacks the competitive advantages and status of major cities like Manchester[175] or Birmingham its multi-faceted and ambitious regeneration strategies suggest that even modest urban locations can become models of good practice[176] in response to technological innovation and the intense competition of other cities.

Salford borders Manchester and has a population of about 229,000. Until relatively recent times it boasted thriving industries in engineering, chemical, brewing and, pre-eminently, textiles. The decline of the last in particular in the decades following World War Two left the city with empty mills, mass unemployment, deteriorating housing stock and a polluted environment. Unemployment is centred in particularly disadvantaged neighbourhoods. In the past decade there has been an increased trend towards part-time working and a significant increase in the banking and finance sector. Manufacturing industries continue to decline. The city has a potential labour force of over 100,000 people, of whom 77,400 are in employment at the time of writing. In addition to relatively high numbers of unemployed people, there are similar numbers of residents who are 'economically inactive'.[177]

Despite the major set backs of the post-war years Salford's urban programmes are imaginative and ambitious. They incorporate action in areas of severe deprivation alongside initiatives geared to the wider city population. Partnership and prescience characterize much of the endeavour with large- and small-scale projects engaging the private and voluntary sectors. These include: a *Disabled Access Guide* for people with disabilities using Salford shopping city; the development of a Resource Centre in a district of Salford called Ordsall, aimed at providing a base for local community groups, and business, training and job search support for local people; and Salford Football Community Link, a city-wide project co-ordinated by the charity NACRO, which helps local communities set up and run junior football clubs.[178]

There is also clear recognition that the future lies not in manufacturing but in pursuing other activities that will exploit the inherent advantages of Salford's location. The long-term strategic vision is set out in the first part of Salford's City Pride mission statement:

> By 2005 . . . Salford will be . . . A European Regional Capital – a centre for investment and growth not regional aid. A city of outstanding commercial, cultural and creative potential. An area distinguished by the quality of life and sense of well-being enjoyed by its residents.[179]

The advantages that in part sustain this vision are twofold: the area has a large dockland of untapped potential and the largest collection in existence of the paintings of L. S. Lowry. In 1996 Salford was awarded a £64 million grant to construct the Lowry Centre, funding coming mainly from the National Lottery and the European Regional Development Fund. Projections suggest that the centre (opened spring 2000) along with the associated developments will generate a further £100 million in private investment, create 6,500 jobs in the retail/leisure sectors, attract 2.5 million visitors and bring in approximately £4 million a year to the locality.[180]

The City Council is also trying very hard to implement a community strategy which develops partnerships between the public, private and voluntary sectors and local communities. The second part of the Salford City Pride mission statement states, 'sustainable regeneration demands that the benefits . . . of development . . . *are experienced within the communities in which they take place* and can be seen to have reference to the lives of the people who live there'. All council services are now managed and delivered on an area rather than a departmental basis. Service users can go to a local area office to sort out problems rather than suffer the frustration of tracking down the right officer or department. All this activity suggests that the pursuit of new economic opportunities is being combined with an inclusive approach to urban renewal that is seeking genuinely to put people first.

Difficult questions remain. First, even with a broadly based strategy it is likely that some local people will see this as another example of tokenism, of the future being shaped by the local authority and related bodies without any real consultation at the level of community leaders or groups. Second, can these bold steps overcome the long-term legacy of urban dereliction? Third, Salford has fared extremely well in its bids for funding: what of the 'losers' (many in equally needy districts) who have been denied funding in order that Salford can be resurrected? And, finally, what about those areas that lack the drive and leadership described here and lack the good fortune of a Lowry collection? All these issues must necessarily form part of the continuing debate regarding the funding, aims and scope of urban policy. What they must not do, however, is stifle projects comparable to those just described. Ambitious in scope, yet fully aware of all the attendant pitfalls, they recall the wisdom of an earlier century that seems just as apposite to the world of action as the life of faith:

> We are so constituted that if we insist upon being as sure as is conceivable, in every step of our course, we must be content to creep along the ground and can never soar. If we are intended for great ends we are called to great hazards; and whereas we are given absolute certainty in nothing, we must in all things choose between doubt and inactivity.[181]

This insight raises the issue of risk and reminds us again that there are always winners and losers in the city. Salford is a good example of an area that is exploiting its innate potential to the full while harnessing technological advances in its bid to be a successful, post-industrial location. Other urban areas, however, have little obvious geographical capital to trade with and are less well placed to take advantage of current economic trends than others. Not all, for example, have local access to universities and colleges to facilitate a stimulating learning environment of interest to new business. Similarly some cities, even with gifted marketing strategies, are severely limited in their capacity to generate a tourist industry. Seven major cities have advanced their claim to be recognized as regional capitals through the 'Core Cities Group' which comprises Birmingham, Bristol, Leeds, Liverpool, Manchester, Newcastle and Sheffield.[182] It is hard to envisage the likelihood of a central policy facilitating equally balanced development across Britain's cities and this opens up the possibility of polarization between not only regions of the country but also individual cities. Quite clearly there is an issue here for the Government in terms of the level of legitimate intervention in this process to offset unacceptable differences which may emerge in the years ahead. Intervention will need to aim at policies balancing local initiatives (and meeting genuine local needs) without entailing huge disparities in levels of funding, particularly when it can be demonstrated that bids from various cities or regions are worthy of equal consideration. The regeneration of the cities is the responsibility of politicians alone but the persistence of the problem and the scale of the funding required to bring about lasting improvements make it inevitable that future government policies, aligned with strategic local participation, will continue to have a direct bearing on the vitality, hopes and human potential of urban communities.

Even if we allow that the cities are capable of facing the challenges of industrial decline, deprivation, economic restructuring and new technology, this still leaves unanswered the questions of social cohesion and human conviviality. When economic developments, consumerism and social breakdown have the power to corrode human relations and the common good can the cities still remain a source of creative and enriching experience?

In his book *Cities of God,* Ward depicts the urban as the interplay of a market that is fixated on consumption and spending.[183] This desire, bordering on obsession, undermines the possibilities of consensus, mutual obligation and interdependence and leads inexorably to a fragmented urban social order characterized by concentrations of poverty and decay where the destitute and the socially damaged are likely to be forgotten. In support of these claims, Ward provides a telling personal anecdote that in its potential range of meanings[184] stands comparison with the Renault Christmas logo described earlier. Once again the context is Manchester, openly publicized as a leading international city of the future.[185]

It was an ugly wet morning, when I came across a body stretched out in the doorway of a functional branch of the UK's leading international bank. Nothing unusual in that – someone sleeping rough. One day walking from one end of Oxford Road to the other I counted seventeen people asking for money, all below thirty years old, some not even in their teens. Among them were four sellers of *Big Issue.* Some sit sprawled across the pavement, some walk from one person to another, some stagger with drink, some lie silent with a notice nearby saying 'Homeless', some are attached to a dog, some beg for money politely, some aggressively, some with a smile and look which suggests payment in kind is available. But what held my attention with this person – who was so completely dug down into a filthy sleeping-bag that there was no telling whether it was a man or a woman, alive or dead – what held my attention here were two objects at the side of the figure. One was a half-finished bottle of Chianti and the other was an old copy of Hegel's *Philosophy of Right* . . . What held my attention was not that this figure might have been me, or any number of academics I know who enjoy a glass of red wine and an intense read about the ethical life, social justice and the state. No, what held my attention was the fact that this scene summed up an enormous cultural fragmentation – bits of life that came from various places seemed tossed together randomly. Everything could be catalogued, itemised, but nothing made sense. An undefined body in a dirty sleeping-bag, a bottle of okay Italian wine, a philosophical classic all out there on the pavement framed by dereliction on the one hand, and international finance on the other, all reduced to the same level not just of banality, but disrespect, degradation.[186]

The anecdote and the argument are to be taken seriously. This chapter has already acknowledged that social marginalization and fragmentation are likely, perhaps inevitable, corollaries of a global market whose benefits are not spread evenly. It is hard to take issue with Ward's contention that the global economics aligned with an ideology of consumption is producing a new urban geography[187] characterized on the one hand by corporate wealth and inflated real estate prices and, on the other, growing poverty and economic inequality:

> Every week new billboards in Manchester, advertise the conversion of erstwhile warehouses, the refurbishment of office space to designer specification, and apartments with luxury fittings. Segmentation, segregation, polarisation, ghettoisation are the flipside of a new gentrification with its demands for designer styles and fashionable accessories . . .[188]

Other social commentators are also pointing to this flipside. A report undertaken for *The Guardian* by Brian Robson of Manchester University notes that cheek by jowl with the new penthouses, restaurants and upmarket stores lies 'the land of the forgotten, . . . the endless rows of impoverished terrace housing and half empty council housing, where unemployment is horrendous . . . Where crime traps people in their homes, where drugs are common currency'.[189] The Chief

Rabbi, Jonathan Sacks, also notes the disturbing divide between different economic classes, the public spaces that have grown fewer and the breakdown of trust that binds communities together.[190] Within this threatening dispensation, Ward is able to contemplate a post-millennium city that is devoid of common ends and purposes and challenges the claim being made here that the emerging urban order may still be regarded as a locus of human flourishing.

At one level we can agree with this sombre reading of the city. That social breakdown and a potential for violence represent part of the urban landscape is not open to question. But once this is conceded, it is then necessary to affirm the many positive elements in an urban crucible that is protean, complex and, crucially, still capable of generating humane values and co-operation. The constitution of cities is not only about the wielding of economic power that brings about alienation and inequality. Whatever the urban landscape represents in terms of money or danger, it is at the same time a place of conviviality, where individuals and groups meet, trade, exchange concerns and ideas. Ward's depiction of the metropolis as the lair of sated yet restless individuals locked inside the dungeons of their egos masks the more prosaic truth that it also represents a place where ordinary people lead their lives and frequently find opportunities for creativity, celebration[191] and kindness. Due acknowledgement needs to be given to the city that is also a place and a space[192] defined by parks, libraries, galleries, street corners, cafés, in fact all the locations that have no ostensible purpose beyond social intercourse, recreation, enjoyment and the fostering of a deeper understanding (cultural, aesthetic or otherwise).

In a lecture Sir Stuart Lipton, Chairman of the Commission for Architecture and the Built Environment, commented:

> Most of us will have some special places that provide respite from the pressures of life, each one like a small oasis. They also have a powerful social function: here people meet, they watch others passing by or children playing; there may be a

conversation, a chance remark; a place where people are comfortable with each other. A civilized environment makes most people feel and behave in a more caring and responsible way, so civility implies less crime, less vandalism, more humanity.[193]

In this respect, not only does Ward exaggerate the alienation that he holds to be a defining characteristic of the urban but also by implication he limits the range of gracious possibilities that at any one time simultaneously contribute to the producing and shape of the modern city and effectively refute his notion that it is nothing more than an impersonal trough of material consumption. His story of the homeless person in Manchester and the social dis-ease it represents constitutes a valid but necessarily attenuated reading of the city. There are other stories.

After the publication of *Staying in the City*,[194] issued to mark the tenth anniversary of *Faith in the City,* I organized a series of meetings[195] in pubs and community centres in Liverpool, Wigan and St Helens with the aim of providing encouragement and informed debate to help clergy cope creatively with the task of urban ministry. The meetings included all denominations, reflecting the original concern of *Faith in the City* that churches in the UPAs should have a clear ecumenical bias. What emerged from the hearings was a sense that UPA clergy perceived themselves to be in situations that were not only challenging but also unique. That parallels exist with forms of ministry in other contexts, rural or suburban, was not disputed. But a clear inference to be drawn from the varied contributions was that urban ministry by virtue of its context, nature and, to a marked degree, the scale of demands made upon it, mark it out for particular consideration. There was a paradoxical awareness of the task as both mundane and frequently debilitating yet also intensely absorbing. Satisfaction came from routine and ritual, as one participant expressed it, 'in the actual calling on people, at all times and under all conditions . . . the coming to grips with the intimate conditions

of their lives'.[196] Reference was made to the experience of
William Carlos Williams the American poet and doctor. Looking back in 1948 over a long general practice, he observed that
his great satisfaction lay in the humdrum, in the million and a
half patients he saw over 40 years. Despite frequent frustra-
tions and disappointments and the human cost of simply
being in a parish or circuit, Williams's insight corroborated
the experiences of those present who pointed to the capacity
for celebration and hope in the midst of suffering and the
generosity of ordinary lives that enabled the city to be spoken
of in terms of gift or privilege:

> In some respects inner-city Liverpool is worse now than at
> the time of the 1981 riots yet despite the vandalism and
> theft what keeps us going is the commitment of ordinary
> people to the Church. We are failing but hanging in there,
> which is faithful to the heart of the gospel.[197]

Two other recollections are personal and shift the backcloth
from Merseyside to New York. On a late Sunday afternoon in
the Autumn of 1999, as I sat in a café on Broadway not far
from the centres of enormous economic power, a steady
stream of children from different ethnic, racial and religious
backgrounds came to the counter to be given free sweets or
chocolates by the assistant as part of the celebrations of
Hallowe'en. There was nothing perfunctory or forced about
the procedure. The assistant was pleasant, the children
graciously received the gift and their accompanying parents
were happy to be sharing in a ritual that brought children,
families and business community together. A small event in
itself, yet against a backcloth of competition and impersonal
market forces, it symbolized the power of the local as a place
of neighbourliness and civility, an opportunity for meeting
rather than just an extension of the market place. A few days
before I had made arrangements to visit a hostel for the homeless run by the cathedral of St John the Divine. A big project
and part of a multi-million social welfare programme run by

the cathedral and financed largely by business corporations. I wasn't quite sure what to expect when I arrived for my appointment (even with my own experience of running such schemes) so I was more than surprised to be greeted by an efficient and busy project manager, coping with the demands of the New York streets yet dressed in full Dracula regalia! Again, Hallowe'en had been made an opportunity for celebration and the expression of human kindness and solidarity in the heart of the city. Atherton comments:

> The local remains the place where global forces now converge and shape the lives of people, communities, associations and environments. Yet it is also a place where they can all, in turn, influence their situations and these forces most sharply and tangibly.[198]

In this chapter we have traced the evolution of the cities in recent years and argued that more and better co-ordination is required in relation to urban projects. Deprivation and decay persist because their root causes have neither been adequately addressed nor understood by the major funding regimes of regeneration.[199] Good reasons have been provided for celebrating the modern city as a place of energy, imagination and resilience that should question the kind of unmerited juxtaposition of the urban with social disorder. Charles Landry has urged a leap in imagination and creativity that will enable us to re-envision what cities are for.[200] He invites us to ponder and dream – an invitation that has already been taken up with passionate conviction by the Australian planner, Leonie Sandercock:

> I dream of a city where action is synonymous with change; where social justice is . . . prized . . . where I have a right to my surroundings and so do all my fellow citizens; where no one flaunts authority and no one is without authority; where I don't have to translate my 'expertise' to impress officials and confuse citizens . . .

I want a city where my profession contributes to all of (this) . . . where city planning is a war of liberation fought against dumb, featureless public space as well as the multiple sources of oppression and domination and exploitation and violence; where citizens wrest from space new possibilities, and immerse themselves in their cultures while respecting those of their neighbours, and collectively forging new hybrid cultures and spaces.[201]

We are to cherish the dream and the multi-faceted textures of the city without, however, becoming unduly sanguine about the health and prospects of the emerging urban order. The problems categorized in this chapter represent a huge task for local and central government and local churches whose commitment to the cities continues to be tested by the financial resources available for its neediest areas,[202] and whose contribution to urban regeneration is necessarily modest in relation to the scale and obduracy of social and economic marginalization. Similarly, globalization, particularly if aligned with more neo-liberal market philosophies, has the power, if unchecked, to exploit the cities and undermine a Christian vision of what a better future might entail.[203] It is not, however, a monolithic and predatory phenomenon, the guise in which it is sometimes portrayed[204] and, increasingly, its dangers are being recognized by influential commentators.[205]

Facing up to globalization, to the *interconnectedness* of our lives, means engaging with change and the problems linked to the international creation of wealth and poverty. It means the ability to understand and critique all the forces – benign or otherwise – that impact upon our urban communities, and determine who has a right to the space of the city.[206] It means working towards a different and more hopeful future for those who are excluded, so that what is done in the city will move things, if only a short space, towards a civilization of love. The next chapter will assess how the churches are responding to these formidable challenges.

4 Discerning the Signs:
A Responsive Church?

The picture so far represents the cities as strategic sites for the convergence of a broad array of social, economic and political processes that makes for wealth and inequality. Writing in *The Financial Times,* Martin Wolf invites its readers to think 'of a stretch limousine driving through an urban ghetto. Inside is the post-industrial world of Western Europe, North America, Australasia, Japan and the emerging Pacific Rim. Outside are all the rest.'[207]

The image of a globalized world characterized by economic disparities and social injustice introduces two questions for the churches. First, how adequate is their theology of the built environment? Is it flexible and big enough to interpret the millennium city and the issues it raises about identity, community and power? Second, to what extent are churches making *strategic* contributions in particular localities and are these consonant with wider Government urban policies that share similar concerns?[208]

The questions are inescapable for four reasons. First, as we noted in Chapter 3, there is the perennial gospel injunction to read the contemporary cultural context in order to discover how best the Christian vision of justice, salvation and the common good might be promoted. Second, this mandate becomes even more urgent at a time of unprecedented change and the continuing marginalization of the churches. For example, with regard to the latter:

Today a churchgoing minority in Britain finds itself located in a society in which only the older generations have been thoroughly nurtured in these beliefs and values. Thus, amongst the fragmentation of post-modernity, weekly churchgoing – for long a minority activity amongst British adults – may now be becoming a culturally isolated activity as well.[209]

Third, we need to examine the extent to which church projects reflect and support wider Government urban policies. *Faith in the City* was clear that the resolution of inner cities' problems required the intervention and specific commitment of central and local government.[210] Fresh initiatives are now under way which indicate that the present Government (2003) is paying increasing attention to these problems while simultaneously offering opportunities to the churches for creative partnerships directed towards urban renewal. As a microenterprise[211] a local congregation has the constructive potential to regenerate its community along with other public service providers and voluntary bodies. Finally – and this is an insight often overlooked – economic systems are influenced by religious values. The Protestant work ethic did much to advance the spirit of capitalism[212] and as far back as the eighth century when Baghdad and Basra became powerful centres of commerce, Islam has contributed to the growth of finance and trade. Piety and self-denial are integral to the religious life but the social order is the arena in which we transform the world and share with God in the work of creation. Historically, Judaism has looked to the market place as the school for sanctification. The Talmud even suggests that the aspiring saint should resist the cloister and opt for worldly holiness by devoting himself to the investigation and pursuit of the ethical laws relating to finance and commerce.

It is for these reasons that the churches must now reassess their role in the dynamics of a global urban culture. This is not simply a matter of faith seeking understanding or how best they might work creatively in partnership with others; it is to concede that the transition from relative strength to dramatic statistical decline[213] in church life now demands a more strategic approach in order that organized mission and worship may continue.[214]

A credible, even urgent, agenda emerges from these initial observations but its priorities and theological presuppositions are contested by some. Not everyone views the urban as a place 'to bring us daily nearer God' and others question the theological propriety of collaborating with strategies that allegedly contribute little to urban communities. So what are the objections?

Anyone with significant experience of working in partnership with Government agencies knows about the bureaucracy and frustration that attend local projects. We persevere, however, because we trust our partners and take the long view – the practical outcomes and benefits to the locality make the effort and anguish worthwhile. But are these assumptions valid? Peter Winn, inner-city priest in the Diocese of Liverpool, comments:

> The Church's contribution to Regeneration Strategies should at least begin with a rigorous questioning of how these initiatives can really bring liberation . . . They do not contribute to the restoration of justice and hope in marginalized urban communities. They operate according to an ideology that destroys human mutuality and actively prevents any challenge to the way society is structured. There is no genuine partnership or consultation and the experts who staff and benefit from the programmes work according to 'Exit' strategies that allow them to plan only for the short term. The Christian community founded on the logic revealed in the Resurrection of the Crucified (1 Cor. 1.17–25) cannot support strategies that do not hope for real transformations.[215]

Winn is right to advocate a critical interrogation of any prospective partnership and the extent to which it will genuinely contribute to local needs and aspirations. Any collective scheme of whatever ideological hue can easily become skewed to serve selfish or political ends. But this should not lead to an entirely pessimistic conclusion concerning political motive or the extent to which genuine local consultation is possible. Referring to recent Government initiatives, Hilary Russell discerns beyond the policy content 'an attempt to develop participative democracy through a re-negotiation of the relationship between the State and the individual in terms of rights and responsibilities'.[216] This is evident in the Neighbourhood Renewal Strategy with its concern to work with local community leaders instead of relying entirely on local authorities that historically have squandered huge financial resources.[217]

Inherent in this approach is the idea of a renewed civil society in which 'partnership makes for better policy making because it increases the stake that individuals have in their community'.[218] The National Strategy for Neighbourhoods has a laudable aim and it seems needlessly cynical to interpret it as a means of bolstering the ideological requirements of government or the prospects of 'generation careerists who are not concerned with the redistribution of power and wealth'.[219] It remains to be seen whether such a raft of initiatives will bring new freedom and opportunities to deprived urban areas but it is worth noting that evidence is already emerging of their benefits as will be shown later in this chapter. In the meantime it is right that they should be subjected to a continuing Christian ethical critique:

> UPA churches remind us that if we want to be faithful to God then we must question what we are told is the 'real world'. And this questioning should not just be a response to specific public crises – where the government tells us we have a part to play – but the continuing insistence that our alternative vocation may not be co-opted and domesticated.[220]

What we should not accept, however, is the charge that

colluding with these partnerships in the interim entails a betrayal of the gospel by effectively settling for the second best.[221] There is no dishonour rendered to the gospel by working with others who are motivated by more than self-interest and opportunism for the sake of the common good and such a stance flows naturally from the Christian doctrines of creation and humanity.[222] It also reflects Temple's conviction that, notwithstanding a tendency to sinfulness, human institutions are still worthy of endorsement because they are integral to the creation and, as such, part of God's own providential order.[223] In consequence, they are able to contribute to the redemption of society and will be assisted in this task by the goodwill and self-giving of those who are animated by the Spirit of Christ.[224]

If the question of regeneration strategies presents a difficulty for some urban practitioners, a broader and more serious issue is raised by those who interpret the city as a location that militates against the sharing of the gospel:

> Like a vampire it preys on the true living creation, alive in its connection with the Creator. The city is dead, made of dead things for dead people. She can herself neither produce nor maintain anything whatever . . . the city devours men.[225]

Jacques Ellul's profound theological pessimism towards the urban order leaves no room for hope or action, beyond the Church living a separate existence within its walls as a counter-cultural movement. The city – like technology for Ellul – contradicts the divine nature of creation and can never become a vehicle for goodness and salvation. There can therefore be no dialogue between the earthly and the heavenly city and the task of theology, as in Biblical times, is to speak only a word of judgement:

> You, mortal, will you judge, will you judge the bloody city? Then declare to it all its abominable deeds. Its officials within it are like wolves tearing the prey, shedding blood,

destroying lives to get dishonest gain . . . The people of the land have practised extortion and committed robbery; they have oppressed the poor and needy, and have extorted from the alien without redress. (Ezek. 22.2, 27–9)

Here, as elsewhere in the Bible, the prophets do castigate the waywardness of the city but Ellul fails to acknowledge that they also on other occasions speak more positively and view the urban with all its moral shortcomings as home to the exile, sanctuary for the stranger and as a place of justice for the persecuted.[226] Taken together the prophetic word of judgement and promise provides a more theologically nuanced interpretation than Ellul's and reflects Temple's view of human institutions as imperfect, yet nevertheless part of a providential dispensation.

A cautionary word is in order here. Temple may have the more balanced theological perspective but currently Ellul is not without followers in the city. Church sub-cultures continue to proliferate with a horror of postmodern society. Within these exclusive households of faith, individuals are offered respite from the world's taint and interpret their marginality as a radical achievement preserving true religion in a milieu that is largely corrosive of Christian values.[227] Apart from Scripture, they are also able to draw on contemporary commentators for support. Alasdair MacIntyre has called for 'local forms of community within which civility and the intellectual and moral life can be sustained through the dark ages which are already upon us'.[228] There is a great chasm between the intellectual world-view of MacIntyre and the sub-cultures described a moment ago but both are concerned to establish communities of resistance in the prevailing darkness.

Resistance of this sort has its theological merits – Judaism, for example, would never have survived in the cities had it allowed itself to be assimilated by the wider culture. The serious weakness of withdrawal, however, lies in the refusal to engage with the complexity of modernity and the legitimate demands it makes upon the Christian conscience. Just as the slum priests of the nineteenth century recognized that to worship the Lord in the beauty of holiness also entailed a readiness to serve him in the poor, no less an obligation is required today:

> Those who believe in a city of God cannot ignore the need for the peace of the earthly city. They cannot collectively withdraw from the responsibility of pursuing the latter into cave or monastery. They share an obligation to be concerned with the state, with justice, with the common pursuit of peace.[229]

A theology which posits the city as a cursed and condemned place and rejects in principle any active attempt to work for its redemption is flawed. Notwithstanding his earlier reservations about the possibilities of human conviviality within the urban, Ward is clear that this form of separation must be rejected on two accounts. First, it is contrary to the Christian doctrines of creation and incarnation and, second, it fails to recognize that Christians are ineluctably wedded to the secular world – they work in it, buy its goods, are susceptible to the lures and demands of the global market. Retreating into privatized communities achieves nothing in terms of healing or salvation and simply leaves the city to rot.[230]

In place of pessimism and withdrawal, Ward, surprisingly it must be said in view of his criticism of *Faith in the City*, comes close to the spirit of the Archbishop's Commission in arguing for an outpouring of love that seeks to transform what is ordinary and mundane. The task of the theologian is to hold on to the vision of better things and to work out, even when confronted by injustice and alienation, how such a future might be realized.[231] Ward not only affirms the theological legitimacy of seeking to redeem the city. His remarks also underpin the need for clarity, for a way of thinking that, on the one hand does not shrink from the complexity of the wider culture and the challenges it presents to urban mission and, on the other, encourages the provision of 'frameworks, strategies, criteria and interventions'[232] that enable local congregations to be the Church in the midst of plurality and change. We are back by a circuitous but necessary route to the questions that opened this chapter. How much evidence is there to show that the churches are genuinely alert to the changing nature of these theological tasks?

From an ecumenical perspective, the most notable contribution has come from the Methodist Church and the publication of its report *The Cities*.[233] It gives considerable space to exploring the context of cities and their most pressing problems with particular reference to urban decay and its associated social problems, homelessness and housing need and transport and related environment issues.[234] Further sections analyse a national survey of what ordinary people think about living in cities today, and the final part offers some theological reflections and recommendations for future action. Under the former, it raises the four themes of creation, incarnation, cross and resurrection, and pilgrimage. In exploring these themes the report acknowledges that it stands within 'a tradition firmly established by *Faith in the City*'[235] and like the Archbishop's Commission finds reasons to celebrate and lament the urban order in all its contrariness, ambivalence and needs:

> The city is both an image of God's presence in creation and also the epitome of human ambition, vanity and greed. It is the product of human creativeness and also the result of an abuse of resources, people and relationships. There are constant tensions between what the city could be and what it is, between the dream and the reality. While Christians may sometimes feel that they do not fully belong to the city, both Scripture and Tradition challenge us to live with this tension. We should wholeheartedly devote ourselves to promoting the welfare of the city in all its parts, despite our discomfort about some of its activities. Christians are always to some extent exiles.[236]

From its findings and consultations,[237] the report depicts the cities as locations of inescapable diversity. The perceptions of those interviewed,[238] for example, reflect the ethos of their neighbourhoods, the ways in which they identify with their area and their listed priorities, which shift significantly according to age, needs and gender.

There is also awareness that cities are caught up in, indeed reflect, the remorseless nature of change and that it will continue to accelerate. The report views the urban future with apprehension, noting on the one hand that globalization and technological innovation represent the most significant development since *Faith in the City* and questioning, on the other, whether any central government will have the political will to secure the cities of the future as viable places within which to live and work. It concludes on a sombre note:

> The introduction to *Faith in the City* (1985) contains the following words: 'Nothing in this report should be interpreted as evidence against our firm belief in an urban future of which all citizens may be proud.' Twelve years later, this Working Group on the cities would have liked to endorse this view, but based on the evidence before us, we find it impossible to be entirely confident about the future of Britain's cities.[239]

The strength of the report is twofold. First, there is its insistence that any examination of the future of the cities must engage with the wider trends that are critically shaping their economic future and the extent to which they enhance or vitiate the quality of life of urban dwellers. Notwithstanding the diversity of urban communities, whether in terms of histories, cultures or religious traditions, what they have in common is a duty to address the great global challenges. Second, there is its commitment to the task of trying to make sense of the city in order to ascertain where its future might lie as a locus of wealth creation and broader social objectives that benefit all within its boundaries. Although some of its recommendations are aimed at local churches and how practical measures might be adopted in pursuit of greater community involvement, its concern throughout is to grapple with what is distinctive about life in the city. In consequence, the report bears witness to the necessity for the Church to listen to voices other than its own and, not least, its own vision of God's relation to the urban:

> It is only when we are moved by the sheer diversity of the city that we feel deeply the experience of God's grace unconditionally among us. That experience creates a new kind of spirituality, which in turn seeks a new kind of theological understanding. If the universe has a human face then so must the city. It is this conviction that has so powerfully influenced the calling of those who might otherwise have fled the city.[240]

The spirit of commitment evoked by these last remarks in relation to the urban can also be found in recent Anglican writings. *Staying in the City* (1995) acknowledges the changes in city life over a decade as well as the persistence of poverty and recommends that priority should continue to be given to UPAs.[241] Unlike the Methodist report however, it makes no serious attempt to grasp the nature and extent of the economic forces now affecting Britain's cities. Similarly, a formal response from the Urban Bishops' Panel to the Government's Social Exclusion Unit as it prepared its report on deprived areas does acknowledge that economic forces beyond specific localities often contribute to urban decline. Global issues, however, are not pursued in any detail.[242] That challenge is now being formally acknowledged: globalization has found its way on to the agenda of General Synod[243] and the Lambeth Conference.[244] The academic community and urban theologians are also providing a forum for policy makers and practitioners keen to explore the role of the Church in relation to the new economic and political context.[245] The synodical report does not offer an incisive analysis of the global market, providing little more than an overview of its challenges and complexities, but it does emphasize the principles of responsibility, local autonomy and control. The essential requirement, it argues, is to engage the market, with its opportunities and threats, and bring to that complex process distinctive Christian insights and values which insist that economics is not simply about information or material gain but also persons with a fundamental need for community.[246]

These useful initiatives suggest the beginning of a debate with regard to the costs and benefits of globalization and its implications for the life and mission of the Church. At the same time, however, they currently represent the fairly narrow worlds of synods and conferences. Is it possible to discern a similar awareness at the grass roots – in dioceses, parishes and circuits – and are local churches thinking and acting strategically in order to make the urban a more just and humane place?

Recent research indicates that, at one level, there is a real and impressive commitment being made across the denominations working in the city that touches groups that other agencies may find hard to reach. The former ecumenical body for churches on Merseyside notes:

> Local churches (nearly 200) meet many of the City's regeneration objectives through their day to day pastoral work and by encouraging their members to take responsibility for each other and their neighbourhoods through involvement in community building activities. They play a major part in supplying the 'glue' for local communities and, to the extent that they have a presence in all parts of the City, they contribute to social cohesion more broadly. In disadvantaged neighbourhoods, where clergy are very often the only professionals living as well as working in the area, they provide a key local facility. They give a round-the-clock social service. They take on many associated leadership roles and are a focus for advocacy about local needs.[247]

Beyond the local, church leaders also provide a voice to communicate the needs of the city and occasionally to speak a word of warning. At a recent conference on retail marketing in Manchester, the Bishop of Liverpool called on planners to 'avoid the disease of urban diabetes, where the blood pumps around prestigious retail and leisure projects in the centre of our cities, but leaves the edges to atrophy and die'.[248]

The overall contribution of the churches and the unpretentious nature of their service is also attracting greater recognition on the part of government and other regeneration agencies. New research has acknowledged the distinctive characteristics and potential that local congregations bring to the urban by honouring Christ's teaching to love your neighbour as yourself.[249] All of this is to the good and demonstrates a high level of organized compassion exercised in Christ's name. Such action is not easy to monitor, however, given the autonomy of local churches and, in some instances, diffuse and uncoordinated policies that are not always integrated with other voluntary organizations in the locality. The duplication of services is sometimes an unfortunate and expensive consequence.[250]

This 'pepper-pot' approach is what churches seem to do best. It looks to practical solutions to urban regeneration and the maintenance of an effective local presence. Data from other sources also suggest that even with regard to dioceses that have formulated urban strategies they tend to cover a wide range of issues usually relating to clergy care and deployment, church buildings, funding and support of church-led community initiatives.[251] Furthermore, as the following examples show, they tend to be couched in general domestic terms, frequently advocating the need for mutual support, interdependence and responsible service.

In June 2000 Southwell Diocese published *Sources of Strength and Hope*.[252] The document runs to 20 pages and has much to say about the need to sustain a prophetic witness in the urban beyond the millennium. It stands in the tradition of *Faith in the City* and frequently makes explicit reference to the report. Significantly, no reference is made to the place of

Scripture, praise and prayer and how these might strengthen congregational life. The omission is curious: like the Archbishop's Commission almost 20 years earlier, it talks about appropriate liturgies but fails to recognize or commend worship as the *raison d'être* of the local congregation. Ford and McFadyen comment:

> It is not by any means accidental that the main focus for Christian identity and community is gathering together to praise and thank God. We do this not only because it is essential for celebrating the heart of faith. It is also vital for enabling personal (and communal) dignity and identity and judging what is right and wrong (and why it is so).[253]

Sources also has nothing to say about globalization or the way it represents a complex backdrop to our increasingly complex lives. It talks about deprivation and exclusion but shows no awareness of the critical and subtle interplay between the global and the local. The same is true of the document's theological presuppositions: they rightly insist on the need for love and justice in relation to the socially marginalized but make no attempt to articulate what it means to live in the contemporary city in relation to order and disorder and how both are to be interpreted theologically. *Sources* represents a useful but limited urban strategy, alert to the continuing need for compassion and the possibilities of creative partnerships with Government initiatives but silent concerning the kaleidoscopic nature of the modern city and its impact on individuals and communities.

Changing Church and Society was published by the Manchester Diocese in 1998. It asks what it means to be the Church in a time of great economic and social change and argues for a strategic involvement by local congregations in their communities so that both retain sustainable futures. A casual reading could interpret its pages as an exercise in institutional self-preservation and the management of inexorable decline. But this is not the case. The promotion of justice and

service to others is emphasized as evidence of authentic
Christian witness to the majority who 'believe without
belonging' to the visible membership of the Church.[254] This
approach affirms and embodies the incarnational dimensions
of the gospel, but whereas traditionally urban clergy and laity
have given selflessly to the local needs with no motive other
than the desire to serve there is now a strategic requirement
that at least part of this service and endeavour should feed
back into the development of the Church.[255] Urban communities and their local churches need each other if they are to
flourish.[256]

Like its Southwell counterpart, *Changing Church and
Society* affirms the primacy of the local – congregations offering their buildings and resources in pursuit of community
development and the provision of pastoral care. Both documents emphasize the need for Christian truth to be embodied
in social action and in partnerships with their communities.
Similarly, both documents point to the importance of theological fundamentals in relation to this task and forms of
Christian nurture that support 'faith, prayer, knowledge and
service'.[257] As a strategic approach to urban mission, however,
Changing Church and Society is more keenly attuned to the
questions that opened this chapter and the need to formulate
an adequate theological response to contemporary urban culture. It shows in detail, for example, how society and Church
have evolved since the 1960s[258] and recognizes the need for
new thinking and appropriate forms of engagement with the
city in contexts that frequently threaten the effectiveness and
survival of organized religion. The tone is not quite apocalyp-
tic, but the message is clear:

> Our report has been produced in the conviction that the
> diocese of Manchester will sink or swim dependent on the
> effectiveness of its engagement with the urban situation.
> And the ultimate test of that lies in its urban priority areas.
> That has been its greatest challenge in the last 200 years,
> and will continue to be so into the next millennium.[259]

Unlike the Southwell report with its tendency towards gener-
alizations and lack of relevant empirical data, *Changing
Church and Society* represents a serious work of reflection by
urban practitioners that offers others in similar situations a
breadth of perspective often unavailable. In its advocacy of
partnerships, for example, the report is clear that the emerging context, by virtue of its nature and challenges, promotes
and requires collaboration that will hold together different
viewpoints, interests and resources.[260] It also recognizes the
increasingly important role of central government, particularly
as it relates to the need for combined efforts to bring about
community renewal at a local level. A working document arising out of *Changing Church and Society* that seeks to promote
and develop its strategic aims comments:

> The need to revisit the questions raised by these reports[261] is
> also inspired by increasing attention being paid by central
> and local Government to problems of deprivation. These
> are giving rise to a proliferation of policies and interven-
> tions to address the issues, most importantly the Urban and
> Rural White Papers (December 2000) and the *National
> Strategy for Neighbourhood Renewal Action Plan* (January
> 2001). Together with key resources developed to inform
> and support new policies, these offer new opportunities to
> increase understanding of the context for mission, to access
> new funding sources, and to play a role in new local
> partnerships.[262]

Changing Church reads like a document that has recognized
the urgency of the hour for the mission and survival of the
urban church. It does not evade the realities of indifference
and decline and is alert to the threats and opportunities now
confronting local congregations at a time when 'neither power
nor influence can be taken for granted and strange alliances
have to be made and deals done from below'.[263] It also raises
again in an acute way the issue addressed earlier – the preparedness or otherwise of Christians to trust Government

regeneration initiatives and engage in conversations and
projects concerning common goals and interests that render
the modern city a place of habitation and promise.[264]

Basic beliefs are at stake here. There is the question of
'political virtue'[265] and the extent to which we think this is still
possible at a time of increasing disillusionment with politics
and in the knowledge that the common good is often blighted
by self-interest, opportunism and short-term thinking. Shortly
before he died the distinguished political journalist Hugo
Young referred his *Guardian* colleagues to Psalm 146 – 'Put
not your trust in princes' – and then urged them to go on fight-
ing the good fight.[266] Like thousands of other readers I was
always hugely impressed by the wisdom and humanity that
informed his journalism, but in this instance whilst endorsing
his mandate to carry on with the struggle I am less sure about
his scriptural injunction concerning our political masters.
Theologically, as the Benedictine teachers of his formative
years would have reminded him, original virtue co-exists in
this world along with original sin and, practically, on the
ground, local regeneration schemes are transforming some
communities for the better. Political decisions, policies and
budgets can make a crucial difference and at the grass roots
voices are now being heard and heeded.

In East Manchester, for example, thousands of council
homes have been transferred from the control of the city council to a new non-profit-making independent housing company,
Eastland Homes. The switch has made possible wide-ranging
repairs and improvements, including better street lighting,
cleaner streets and the introduction of alley gates made by
local men at a nearby ironworks. The regeneration has been
facilitated by the New Deal for Communities strategy and the
vision of two local women who have lived in the area for years
and are members of the Eastland Homes Board. Here is
Barbara Taylor's assessment:

> The government's initiatives have been resident-led and for
> the first time we have been asked to be involved rather than

having things imposed on us. We have been empowered instead of being spoken to like idiots. The council spends millions of pounds a year in this area and people can't see where the money has been spent. What the New Deal for Communities (another government programme for regenerating run-down areas) does is get A working with B and B working with C – it is about the different agencies working together. We might not be Einsteins, but we know about our areas, we know what the problems are and we know what people are saying.[267]

These initiatives represent good news for a community that had lost any sense of civic pride and was then surprised to find itself in genuine conversations with senior government ministers that led to a more hopeful future. Politics remains the art of the possible and at the local level it will, quite properly, frequently translate into the adequacy or otherwise of bricks and mortar that 'will make people want to live here'.[268] Any serious urban strategy contemplated by the churches calls for a careful analysis of the underlying rationale of regeneration schemes but I want to argue that it also requires a real appreciation and understanding of what politicians are trying to do and are actually able to do.[269] Bricks and mortar do matter an awful lot to an awful lot of people and it is worth recalling that on the evidence of its original research, the Archbishop's Commission was clear that no presentation of the gospel was possible that did not specifically address material deprivations for the reason that they 'dominated people's thinking'.[270]

None of this is to suggest that the gospel or regeneration schemes will make their mark just by concentrating on the tangible. Communities begin to flourish when politicians and local people recognize the obligation we owe to each other and the extent to which many apparently intractable problems are at root problems of relationships – the networks that form locally, what moves individuals to trust each other and what makes them co-operate and feel fulfilled.[271] More will be said on these issues in Part Three.

The two questions that opened this chapter asked whether the churches possess an adequate theological framework to make sense of the modern city and a strategic approach to help secure the future of local urban communities. If we take the second question first, the diverse and socially useful activities identified in the previous pages are clearly contributing to community development. The imaginative and principled activities of local congregations confirm on the one hand that Christian truth embodied in social action is very persuasive and, on the other, that such action sometimes leads to wasted resources and a failure to share experience on pressing social issues with other agencies. An absence of developed strategies not only diminishes the opportunities for faith communities and dioceses to play a fuller part in the development and implementation of Government social policy in the cities[272] but also confines church initiatives to the issues of survival and effectiveness. Both have to be addressed for the reasons advanced earlier but they also help to explain why urban mission has yet to grasp the far-reaching implications of globalization. We are back to question one.

At the grass roots, congregations and their leaders must now develop a new awareness of the twenty-first-century imperative to think globally and act locally. Behind the deceptive simplicity of the slogan lies the requirement for prayerful and sustained reflection on how power, influence and vested interests define the texture, quality and prospects of urban living and the ways in which organizations, institutions and policies shape individual lives and the possibilities of social justice. These are not merely theoretical considerations. What is at stake is the future of the city and our preparedness to ask questions of global capitalism for the sake of a more humane urban order. The task, admittedly, appears daunting. Once it was easier to recognize what was going on. But not any more, not when connections between agents become more tenuous and less obvious and corporations seem more shadowy and less accountable. Yet even when the difficulty of the undertaking is conceded there is, undeniably, something exciting and absorbing in trying to make sense of globalized urban living. There is also a price to pay for the failure to embrace this new requirement:

> I want to suggest that a church that fails to realize its potential in this new context will find itself more and more reduced to individualistic pietism and dogmatic introspection. The strengths of the Church must lie in its ability to hold the local and the global in its own dynamic tension, as it seeks the practice of human freedom in the presence of God in whatever human arrangements it encounters at local, national, regional and global levels. The Church needs to understand and realize its potential as it connects and affirms the communities and individuals in the margins of the global city . . . While challenging the reshaping of the geography of power, the Christian faith is lived through presence(s), through communities that include, strengthen and give integrity to those at the margins. Local pastoral praxis becomes simultaneously global political praxis.[273]

We have already noted that a preoccupation with personal piety combined with the refusal to engage modernity (for whatever reason) negates the best impulses of Christian faith and conscience. It compounds the prejudices of other partners in the city who wish religion to remain in the private sphere because it is socially divisive[274] and it fails to 'listen, learn and dialogue with those communities whose lives are being shaped by many forces, flows and interests'.[275] The complexities of the twenty-first century and the fragile futures of the marginalized who live within its boundaries demand and deserve better than this. In Part Three I will offer some suggestions for those who wish to renew their contract with the urban and require appropriate theological and spiritual resources for this disciplined task.

Part Three

Strategies for the City

5 A Big Enough Theology

Following an encounter with a minister in a notorious Victorian parish, Matthew Arnold was moved to write:

'Twas August and the fierce sun overhead
Smote on the squalid slums of Bethnal Green,
And the pale weaver, through his window seen
In Spitalfields, looked thrice dispirited.

I met a preacher there I knew, and said:
'Ill and o'erworked, how fare you in this scene?'
'Bravely', said he, 'for I late have been
Much cheer'd with thoughts of Christ, the living bread'.[276]

Arnold reminds us that urban mission has a long and distinctive tradition characterized by a readiness to serve and a lively hope focused upon Christ. Faith in action has been a recurring theme throughout these pages. With one eye we have read of much good work on the part of local Christians as they stand alongside the poor and marginalized, symbolizing a dogged refusal to countenance apathy or cynicism as the only possible responses to change and decline. With our other eye we have also been made aware of the problematic dimensions of inner-city church life and the difficulty of sustaining a Christian vision. Arnold's 'squalid slums' are, thankfully, much less evident. Poverty and hopelessness, however, still permeate the urban landscape as congregations struggle to maintain their cohesion, identity and purpose in a largely secular context. Callum Brown notes that since 1963,

a formerly religious people have entirely forsaken organized

Christianity in a sudden plunge into a truly secular condition . . . What emerges is a story not merely of Church
decline, but of the end of Christianity as a means by which
men and women, as individuals, construct their identities
and their sense of 'self'.[277]

The obituary notice seems somewhat premature set against
the high levels of belief in God revealed by the recent census
and public expectations of the churches when individuals,
communities or the nation come to terms with tragedy and
death.[278] Yet Brown is surely on firmer ground once we
acknowledge the continuing dramatic decline in churchgoing,
the widespread ignorance of, or indifference to, fundamental
Christian doctrines and the disquieting fact that the 'language
of God, once quite common in public life . . . is now muted, if
not almost silent'.[279]

Any discussion of the future of urban mission has to reckon
with this wider cultural context – the mutation[280] of religion in
a society increasingly dominated by consumerism and pick-
and-mix spiritualities[281] and an era characterized by interdependence and rapid communication. The world is our concern
and competing ideas and values (even those that are corrosive
of Christian belief) remind us of the perennial task of discipleship:

The Church is ever ailing and lingers on in weakness,
'always bearing about in her body the dying of the Lord
Jesus that the life also of Jesus might be made manifest in
her body'. Religion seems ever expiring, schisms dominant,
the light of the Church dim, its adherents scattered.
Meanwhile, this much of comfort do we gain from what has
been hitherto – not to despond, not to be dismayed, not to
be anxious at the troubles which encompass us. They have
ever been; they shall ever be; they are our portion.[282]

Newman was writing on the eve of what in fact proved to
be a great spiritual awakening in modern British Church
history.[283] Like Arnold he brings us wisdom from the past: the

Church is free to remain a community of hope sustained on the one hand by the knowledge that as the extension of the body of Christ on earth it must bear its title deeds of cross and resurrection and, on the other, by the conviction (admittedly, often faltering) that the future belongs to God. In that unfolding dispensation, households of faith have a measure of freedom to create better tomorrows because the future is not written.[284]

What is genuinely remarkable in this respect is the extent to which local urban churches remain significant players as microenterprises and voluntary organizations, despite the fact that they often command the active support of only a minority of people. To borrow a phrase from the political philosopher Edmund Burke, congregations are 'little platoons'[285] – intermediate institutions that help to sustain the fabric of civic and social life while simultaneously displaying a level of utility that often exceeds any reasonable expectation of what might be achieved in the city by small, voluntary gatherings. This utility amounts to more than just a humane response to the demands of compassion. At its best it may also be understood as a form of self-giving that makes actual again the divine love that in Jesus visibly expended itself for the sake of others.[286] In Moltmann's words, this represents a preparedness on the part of the local church to identify with its suffering Lord – to be 'drawn into his self-surrender, into his solidarity with the lost and into his public suffering'.[287] It is also to believe the words that Jesus spoke to his followers 'The works that I do, you shall do and greater still' (John 14.12).

Pondering these words, my mind turns to an obituary I came across again a few days ago in a research file. Patrick O'Mahoney was parish priest of Our Lady of the Wayside in Birmingham until his death in 1991. There he formed the first church-based Amnesty International Group. One Christmas 9,000 cards went from the parish to prisoners of conscience in 24 countries. Quite uniquely the church stored medicine and drugs for Third World emergencies and in an international crisis O'Mahoney would charter a plane and fill it with procurements provided free by local manufacturers. In a commitment that involved 34 countries, medical help and disaster relief amounting to the value of between a quarter and half a million pounds was sent *each* year from a parish that conspicuously lacked wealth or influence.

O'Mahoney also made a study of the ethics of investment which led his archdiocese to disinvest from 13 multinationals with bad records overseas and from 3 local companies because of their poor employment practices. He was a remarkable priest who in the throes of all this activity and at the age of 63 completed a PhD thesis based on a comparative study of the ethics of genetics. His disciplined energy and determination enthused others around him: the congregation continued to learn and its people demonstrated to a much wider constituency what Jesus meant when he said that the kingdom of God is already present in our midst. The obituary notice contains his photograph: from underneath a rather crumpled tweed hat, a strong and compassionate face peers out with eyes that challenge, even interrogate, the reader. They suggest to me that Patrick O'Mahoney understood something quite fundamental about the missionary task. An excess of passion of itself, even for the high cause of the kingdom, is never enough. Although he gave himself unstintingly to the cares, hopes and fears of his locality, he retained a global vision, influenced perhaps by his father, a merchant seaman who had seen degrading poverty in India and Africa. O'Mahoney read extensively, thought deeply and wrote perceptively. His tutored moral sense led him to see that, in his own words, 'the infringement of human rights anywhere was the concern of people everywhere'. His support of the Medical Foundation for the Victims of Torture was just one example of where his concerns lay and where his mind followed.

There has been no shortage of passion or activity among urban churches in recent years but as one commentator has noted 'sometimes we suffered from having more passion than analysis and understanding . . . vastly underestimating the urban complexity by which we were confronted'.[288]

The *interconnectedness* of things – social, political and economic – calls for fresh theological presuppositions and priorities in order to comprehend and address the dizzy effects of change and their global character. This is not to argue that the old ways were wrong: in what follows great importance will be attached to the familiar themes of worship and community service. And I am not suggesting that in relation to the way forward all that matters is strategic thinking. To be too precise or prescriptive in relation to the direction of urban mission is 'to leave little reason or scope for the continuing process of prayer and the discernment of God's will'.[289] This view seems sound and the remaining chapters will emphasize the importance of prayer and spirituality as integral elements within a renewed commitment to the urban.

Unashamedly, however, I do want to encourage the practice of thinking – primarily because it is a moral activity. Clarity of thought helps us to discern what is actually going on and is therefore an exercise in truth seeking. The philosopher Iris Murdoch used to say that she preferred the 'hard idea of truth to the facile notion of sincerity'. A little harsh perhaps and as a maxim easily misunderstood. Her concern, however, was to warn against the notion that because we are sincere about something it does not follow that we are either right or working to the best end. Hard thought exposes our own confusions and prejudices (often obscured by relentless activity in pursuit of good causes)[290] and is one way of re-ordering priorities for mission. It can assist the task of 'reimagining the city' in order to see where the creative possibilities and pressure points genuinely lie. And for overbusy urban practitioners driven by complex bundles of beliefs and desires and susceptible to the stress and weariness associated with contexts where frequently there is so little time and so much to do it may provide one way of responding more effectively to the seminal issue of what the post-millennium city represents and what it could or should represent in the future. I recognize from my own experience of urban ministry the distractions and temptations that militate against this disciplined approach. But I can also testify to its benefits and practical outcomes. The great reforming Labour politician Barbara Castle was once told, 'Think, think, think. It will hurt like hell at first but you will get used to it.'[291] We have to do the same. Religion is the deepest form of life and our engagement with the city requires an educated heart and a passionate mind – something that Patrick O'Mahoney understood and practised very well. In short it calls for a big enough theology and forms of local practical discipleship through which 'the Christian community embodies and enacts its fundamental vision of the gospel',[292] a gospel that is also capable of gaining a hearing in the public arena and has something to say to those from other disciplines and agencies with different convictions but common interests in relation to contemporary urban issues.[293] Four theological principles form the basis of this new approach.

A reformulated urban theology should be a *public theology* with the ability to command attention as one distinctive contributor among others to public discourse.[294] Important questions arise here regarding identity, aims and method that will be considered later. It should also be committed to the principle of *partnership* in order at one level to confront the issue of continuing urban decline and, at another, to engage with organizations that have no religious affiliations and other non-Christian faith communities. This stance recognizes that no one agency – voluntary, business, religious or state – can satisfactorily address or explain the complexities of the economic and social fortunes of the city. There are insidious dangers in this approach, particularly the threat to Christian distinctiveness that can arise when the preparedness of theology to take the contemporary world seriously results in the world setting the agenda. Thiemann comments:

> Too often theologies that seek to address a broad secular culture lose touch with the distinctive beliefs and practices of the Christian tradition . . . In the process, the distinctive substance and prophetic 'bite' of the Christian witness are undermined.[295]

A third requirement therefore is that a reformulated urban theology should be grounded in a *disciplined spirituality* that helps to reinforce Christian identity while simultaneously providing the depth and perspective that make possible a tutored reading of the city. Finally, urban mission should *rethink its approach to the margin* – viewing it as a place that can make a difference to the surrounding culture rather than a location of irrelevance or weakness.[296]

The roots of a public theology can be traced back to the nineteenth-century and the conviction of F. D. Maurice that we serve our times best by taking seriously the questions raised by its citizens.[297] *Faith in the City* was moved by the same spirit. In either case it is clear that theology can and should make a constructive and critical contribution to public debates and policies.[298] But what is meant now by public theology and to what extent does it differ from the thinking of *Faith in the City* and its creative engagement with the social order two decades ago?

In answer to the first question, a public theology that has traditionally concerned itself with issues of social justice, power and culture should now be big enough to embrace and interpret a variety of concerns in a way that is commensurate with the 'plural, multi-faceted, multi-causal nature of the world we live in and its problems'.[299] The key word here is *commensurate* – that is to say the broadest of visions that is aware of and responsive to matters of public import.[300] Let me try and earth this in a research visit I made to New York in the Autumn of 1999. During my stay at Union Theological seminary I made contact with the School of Social Work at Columbia University – barely a stone's throw from the seminary. The two institutions offer joint programmes that enable students to address the intricacies of urban life. Here is the synopsis of Course T7124 on Macro Community Practice:

This course is designed to critically examine how social agencies interface with major community actors – government, non-profit, and business agencies and how they

network and co-ordinate their programs across agency
lines. In addition, how agencies affirm their service mission
in the community through marketing and public relations;
how clients and constituents are involved in organizational
governance; and how boards and lay leaders are recruited
and prepared to take on their overseeing responsibilities.[301]

The course clarifies how contextual analysis represents an
attempt to understand the dynamic interaction between social
structures and culture. During a meeting with Debra Jenkins,
Assistant Director of Student Services in the School of Social
Work at Columbia, she commented: 'It is essential that urban
churches should understand the systems within which they
operate – not least, the short-termism that inevitably affects
many political decisions.'[302]

Jenkins is a seasoned urban practitioner who in her former
role was employed as an assistant to the President of the
New York City Development Corporation where she had
access to how a world city is shaped and produced. The
experience has not made her unduly cynical but she remains
convinced that realism must inform the reflections and mission of the churches if they are to operate effectively in the city.
Almost certainly, if we were in conversation now she would
be questioning me about Ground Zero and the adequacy, or
otherwise, of our theological response when an attempt is
made to destroy a world city rather than create it. The aftermath of 9/11 and the fall of the World Trade Centre – that day
when millions of tons of steel, concrete, glass and human
remains fell like ghastly snow on lower Manhattan – has produced a range of theological perspectives. Their emphases differ but in each case there is an evident concern to understand
the event, partly because of its social and political magnitude
but also out of a conviction that the 'God we worship sustains
everything that is: there is ultimately therefore a theological
interpretation of everything that happens in life'.[303] In the
same way that Jewish theologians anguished over the presence
or absence of God in the Nazi death camps some writers have

raised again the age-old question of theodicy – of how a belief
in a loving and all-powerful God can be reconciled with events
that seem to negate such an affirmation,[304] an important question but not I think the heart of the matter in this particular
tragedy.

More recently Dr R. William Franklin, formerly Dean of
the Berkeley Divinity School at Yale, and the church historian
Mary Donovan have conducted a series of interviews with
people who survived the terrorist attack.[305] The stories inevitably constitute painful and illuminating reading and reveal the
ability of the human spirit to endure and learn in a time of
pestilence. The final section of the book does not speculate
on the problem of evil but demonstrates the significance of
basic Christian acts and principles – sacraments, compassion,
priesthood, the use of suffering and the hope of resurrection in
the rubble of the New York streets. The twin towers were
located within the Episcopalian parish of Trinity. The parish
chapel, St Paul's, survived intact and became a centre for
workers and rescuers and a living symbol of the God who in
the New Testament goes down into the grave and then returns
from the pit of darkness and despair. As the book's title – *Will
the Dust Praise You?* – makes clear the stories and reflections
represent a spiritual response to 9/11 and they help us to find
some theological truth in the dust and carnage of the day that
changed the modern world. But they are concerned with individuals, their hurts, griefs, doubts and destinies – matters of
sympathy and human solidarity in the face of the unspeak-
able.

To locate a distinctive voice that looks beyond the immediate
pastoral and spiritual concerns of 9/11, that, in other words,
shifts the theological perspective to a wider public arena, we
can look to Rowan Williams, now Archbishop of Canterbury
but then in conference a mere block away from the World
Trade Centre as the planes impacted. His little book *Writing
in the Dust: After September 11*[306] may be read as a personal
testimony and an attempt to understand what happened in the
dust of the streets that morning. The title evokes the figure of

Jesus who when confronted with an adulterous woman (John 7.55; 8.11) knelt to write in the dust with his finger, refusing to punish or condemn her. Williams invited the same restraint from a nation now looking to its security and to a settlement with the evil forces behind the massacre. It was a plea that any reckoning with September 11 has to be set in the context of a world still awash with human misery and injustice – where on a day that 3,000 people perished in New York and Washington, another 40,000 children died needlessly across the globe, victims of oppression, poverty and famine.[307] It was also, by implication, a terse reminder that the United States and the West generally could not escape some responsibility for a hostile world that generates terrorist atrocities.[308]

Public theology after 9/11 must therefore be mindful of the growing gap between the richest and poorest in the world and the potential this creates for resentment or rage on the part of all those who are excluded. It must also be deeply concerned with the underlying questions of how and why some are affluent and millions remain destitute. The latter, like those in the gospels loved and accepted by Jesus, are not responsible for their plight and yearn to hear redemption's song that will lead them into fuller life. They constitute a great global challenge that calls for the moral and mental acuity of local church leaders like Patrick O'Mahoney who are 'prepared to discern the key issues and think through Christian responses to them'.[309] Such a task will be informed and illuminated by a serious engagement with the accumulated wisdom of the Christian past [310] and a readiness to encounter the rich cultural, social and religious diversity of other groups and institutions.[311]

The guiding principle here is that of partnership – people and organizations working together to achieve more than they would in isolation. *Faith in the City*, it is important to recall, endorsed this approach and recommended that it should be developed by central and local government 'to promote greater consultation with, and participation by, local people at neighbourhood level'.[312] The recommendation indicates the need to move beyond the language of servanthood that has been such a prominent feature of incarnational theology in order to affirm new forms of relationship within the urban. Drawing on his ecumenical experience, Raymond Fung offers a theological rationale for this innovative way of working and also considers some of its practical implications:

> The concept of the Church as servant to the world no longer communicates today. The new language proposed in the ecumenical strategy for Christian witness is partnership. The local congregation sees itself as a partner with the people in the community, and offers itself publicly as such . . . The concept of partnership is a distinct and unmistakable echo of Jesus' way of dealing with his fumbling followers. At one point, he said to them: 'I no longer call you servants because a servant does not know his master's business; instead I have called you friends; for everything that I learned from my Father, I have made known to you.' (John 15.15)[313]

I have to say that Fung's opening remark that 'the concept of the Church as servant to the world no longer communicates today' does not reflect my own experience of urban mission where, repeatedly, the readiness of a local church to offer its own resources, including its physical presence and own sense of vulnerability in pursuit of the common good, can often serve as its main credential. The following extract from a letter to *The Church Times* makes the point well:

> Sir, I am vicar of an urban-priority-area parish near the centre of the town. My parish is often labelled as a den of crime, drug-dealing, and intimidation. The vicarage is in the most disadvantaged part of the parish, and stolen cars are regularly burnt out close by. My family and I may have felt some uneasiness from time to time, but we have never been threatened; we have had only one minor theft, and the church building adjacent to us has never been damaged during our time here. Instead, the community tend to

protect us and respect the Church. One of the reasons for this is precisely because the vicar lives among the people whom he serves. I cannot express just how important this is to the parishioners. Because the Church tries its best to stand alongside them, they identify with it; there is a real sense of communal ownership.[314]

Fung's reference to John's Gospel to underpin the case for partnership also needs to take account of Scripture's recognition of service as a paradigm of Christian leadership. The New Testament argues for many gifts as the legitimate marks of ministry but responsible service is especially prominent in the teaching of Jesus and Paul and a necessary corollary of faith in the epistle of James. As Northcott comments:

The sayings of Jesus include many references to leadership as service including the dramatic image of the Lord washing his disciples' feet and many warnings against patterns of leadership which ape the dominating and oppressive style of leadership in society at large. (Mark 10.42–5)[315]

A little later in the same passage, however, Northcott also goes on to argue that the success of the mission to the Gentiles owes much to the notion of the apostles as fellow workers who are exhorted to work as a team[316] to foster and further the new community of relationships which has been instituted through the resurrection of Jesus.

These two caveats apart, a reformulated urban theology will embody the principle of partnership by acknowledging the importance of interdisciplinary work, practical collaboration and learning from others. In a modest way *Faith in the City* points to the necessity of all these undertakings. But there is little by way of theological underpinning in its recommendations and, even less, any sense of the increasing plurality of the world that necessarily requires greater local co-operation. By contrast, a big enough theology will seek to incorporate three distinctive features.

A Social God

Surprisingly, the doctrine of the Trinity is not mentioned in the theological priorities of *Faith in the City*. In relation to partnership this omission is regrettable. As contemporary writings[317] have demonstrated, the understanding of God as Three Persons yet one God, as a social God, has direct relevance to the vocation of urban mission to be firmly rooted in the life of the world. The recent Methodist report on the cities notes the relevance of the doctrine of the Trinity for our thinking about God's relation to humanity 'especially in its most problematic form, the city'.[318] The *Turnbull Report* on the structures of the Church of England also states:

> The Church is the body of those who believe in the Son, and, as his bride, is the object of the Son's own love. We live out of the resources which God in his love has promised and given, by the Holy Spirit shed abroad in the hearts of the faithful. The life of the Church, in a rich and yet mysterious way, is thus utterly Trinitarian in its ground, hope and being.[319]

Both quotations imply a broad sacramental understanding of the Church that is comprehensive enough to reflect what is done in the name of Christ in the city, and points to the local church as a sign of Christ's presence in the world, a sacrament of divine grace and outward human structure.[320] They also suggest that God can best be known through the experience of mutuality and authentic relationships. Just as Father, Son and Holy Spirit give equal glory to each other within the communion of the Trinity, an urban theology is able to extend this principle of divine mutuality to the life of the local church. As the Orthodox theologian J. Zizioulas has expressed it 'being means life and life means communion'.[321] Giving and receiving, however, are not to be confined only to the household of faith. The element of mystery within the Trinity that serves as a symbol of transcendence – of the Otherness of God – entails

that communion as a way of life and form of mission is much
more than the fellowship of a local congregation. It extends
beyond church boundaries to wider partnerships for it
acknowledges that God as trinitarian mystery, as the ultimate
source and sustainer of all things, is not to be confined to any
one privileged sphere – religious or otherwise. This again is
something that Orthodox theology articulates rather well
with its insistence that although God may not be known in his
essence, his energies are dispersed throughout creation. It is
through these energies that the divine life manifests itself. If, as
Gerard Manley Hopkins wrote, the whole world is charged
with the grandeur of God then it follows that the possibilities
of communion exist at every turn and in unexpected alliances.
The words of Jesus would seem to support this view: when
told that his family stands waiting to speak to him he asks,
'Who is my mother and who are my brothers?' And then
pointing to his disciples declares, 'Here are my mother and my
brothers. For whoever does the will of my Father in heaven is
my brother, sister and mother' (Matt. 12.48–50).

The Necessity of Dialogue

The notion of a social God therefore requires us to acknowledge that the principle of partnership should be extended to
forms of dialogue with other faith traditions, Christians or
otherwise:

> In a global society Christians are invited to take shared
> responsibility with those of other faiths for peace, justice,
> the preservation of creation and a renewed ethic. The fate of
> the earth is the concern of all human beings regardless of the
> religion or world-view to which they adhere.[322]

A commitment to dialogue is not just a matter of ecological
prudence but arises out of the prior recognition that, in a
global context, a developing religious faith is now about constructing new patterns of understanding through dialogue

with others. In this respect the Archbishop's Commission saw ecumenical partnership as an integral element of the Christian response to God.[323] The potential for grass-roots ecumenism is, however, still largely untapped. A renewed approach to the venerable principle of 'not doing alone what can best be done together'[324] could bring dividends to all UPA churches as they serve their communities and learn from each other.[325] Rita Maria Trucious, Director of Community Care at the Episcopal Cathedral of St John the Divine, New York, commented 'the more we share, the stronger we are',[326] emphasizing that although weakness is a paradoxical virtue of the Church it can also be a debilitating and dispiriting feature of urban ministry. Robert (Bobby) Castle, Rector of St Mary Episcopal Centre in Harlem was even more adamant:

> Ecumenism is something we must do at the practical level and seminarians must be taught the principles of organizing with others for the sake of the gospel. Availability is fine but organization is the key to an effective presence in the city.[327]

With regard to interfaith dialogue, *Faith in the City* confined itself to the theological problems presented by non-Christian traditions, the need to respect their integrity and the cautious advocacy of a 'more open approach while ascribing ultimate authority to the claims of Jesus Christ'.[328] The one unequivocal endorsement of dialogue comes almost as an afterthought:

> Our responsibility for the community is one that we also share with other religious bodies. As we seek to exercise it together we grow in mutual understanding and respect; and when people of different faiths find opportunities for practical collaboration and mutual discussion they begin to discover for themselves the riches of our shared humanity and the solidarity created by our common quest for God.[329]

It is also significant that the motivation for dialogue arises out of a shared concern for the community. There is no explicit recognition of the fact that a new and rapidly changing global context and the potential of religion for conflict[330] or reconciliation within it now demands humility and a greater willingness to learn from representatives of other religious traditions.[331] Ward writes perceptively and movingly of a context in which Christendom is over and how the new dispensation of the city with its shifting networks and complex relations entails that 'Christianity . . . is continually defining itself, on the one hand, *against* other positions and, on the other, *with respect* to other positions':[332]

> I live with my Jewish neighbour, I eat with my Muslim friend, I listen with the Quaker who sits and listens with me, and I slowly learn about the religions of South Asia . . . I can and do remain a Christian, but my body is continually mapped onto other bodies . . . We must necessarily make judgments with regards to all sorts of things and we must, with equal necessity, confess our ignorance. We must suspend our judgment about those who pursue love, mercy, justice and righteousness in other practices and in other communities with other liturgies and symbolic exchanges. We must sink ourselves deeper into our own traditions, meditating upon the grammar of faith we live . . . and not be afraid that others do things differently . . . in the urban spaces we share and produce . . . The real questions about the relation of different faith communities and traditions only emerge as we learn to live together without fear.[333]

The tact and openness that may lead us to a more comprehensive awareness of the energies and activities of God beyond the boundaries of the Church also needs to be complemented by a growing understanding that partnership is about identity as well as dialogue. Ward does not advocate a liberal blurring of faith perspectives but challenges us to be more confident and clear about our own. In this way conversation with those who inhabit other theological worlds will be recognized as opportunity instead of threat.

Christian Identity

Partnership and dialogue in a global context raise in an acute way the issue of 'what Christ means in it and for it'.[334] It calls us back to another perennial gospel task – that of delineating an appropriate vision of Christ for this time and no other that calls for 'subtle adjustments, both conscious and unconscious, to the boundaries of our Christology which we have inherited from those who in their generation used their imagination in a similar way'.[335] Mary Warnock has described this as a 'continuum of imagination',[336] the careful reflection and imaginative vigour that is brought to bear on the traditions we inherit that point to the centrality and mystery of Christ in the redemption of the world. As urban culture evolves with its amalgam of new experiences and questions, so too are new aspects and features of Jesus discovered if we recognize on the one hand that our grasp of 'who Christ really is for us today'[337] is always partial and, on the other, that further illumination comes only through a deeper engagement with the mystery of his Person. The final paragraph of what is perhaps the most remarkable book of the twentieth century about Jesus merits inclusion here:

> He comes to us as One unknown, without a name, as of old, by the lakeside, He came to those men who knew Him not. He speaks to us the same word: 'Follow thou me!' and sets us to the tasks which He has to fulfil for our time. He commands. And to those who obey Him, whether they be wise or simple, He will reveal himself in the toils, the conflicts, the sufferings which they shall pass through in His fellowship, and, as an ineffable mystery, they shall learn in their own experience Who He is.[338]

Schweitzer's mesmerizing picture of One who is with us yet

always beyond us, always calling us to risk and struggle and learn, seems to me still fresh and compelling almost a century on. And it is a timely corrective to urban theologies that have too carelessly affirmed the secular city with little reference to Christ, as One in whom all things hold together.[339] Here is a famous example:

> The Gospel does not summon men back to dependency, awe and religiousness. Rather it is a call to imaginative urbanity and mature secularity . . . The issues upon which it must centre are none other than the life and death issues of the secular metropolis. It must be reflections on how to come to political terms with the emergent technical reality which engulfs us. These are political issues and the mode of theology which must replace metaphysical theology is the political mode.[340]

Cox is still exciting to read but he manages to disregard the extent to which the emerging urban order renders his secular Christian values indistinguishable from consumerism and capitalism. His scant references to Christ are solely for the purpose of reminding us that, through Jesus, God teaches us to get along without him in order to become mature and fully human.[341] Thirty years later we know better: urban mission requires us to hold fast to Christ and to follow him as the source of our hope and identity as we ponder where to begin and what to do in this time of *interconnectedness* where everything interacts with everything.[342]

If we are to make the right sort of connections in such an exciting yet bewildering context, our thinking and partnerships and, no less, our faithful response to Christ as a costly way of living[343] will all need to be grounded in a disciplined spirituality that nurtures Christian distinctiveness and helps us to recognize what is possible under God amid the competing claims of the urban landscape. Overbusyness or its corollary exhaustion in the face of too much complexity or human need blur our vision and can give rise to quiet desperation. A disciplined spirituality is a form of resistance to these debilitating tendencies and a vital element in Christian formation centred on prayer, Bible study and the practical knowledge necessary for urban mission, informed by a careful reading of the city. It has to do with the disposition of the soul geared towards making connections in the market place, a particular kind of orientation and practice which Anderson defines as a *habitus*. This is

> not just about thinking and it is more than skills. It is like learning how to do theology by heart. It is as close to us as breathing. It transcends the distinctions between intellect and affect that have often divided approaches to what is essential for ministry.[344]

Underpinning this rather difficult concept is a plea for the integration of heart and mind that is in turn corroborated by distinctive forms of practice and reflection. Certain implications follow: skills and informational learning are by themselves not enough. We have to seek a deeper engagement with the Scriptures and traditions that we seek to live by and that furthermore affirm the urban as a location with a recognizably human purpose under God. This will call us back to the tales that Jesus told, the public arena where he confronts the political and religious powers of Jerusalem and the marginalized he invites to a new way of life – what one New Testament scholar describes as the 'kingdom of nobodies and nuisances'.[345] It will also safeguard against the conducting of theology as merely an intellectual exercise and point to the importance of spirituality as a source of theological reflection.[346] A big enough theology of the city therefore will be a performative discipline committed to, and authenticated by, its solidarity with the lost yet always seeking to ground this in prayer, silence and stillness.[347]

   This form of life at one level is a movement towards a deeper level of intensity that has little to do with emotion and is intimately connected to prayer and the silence beyond words towards which all genuine praying moves. Although D. H. Lawrence is not normally regarded as a religious writer the following lines seem very pertinent to the business of prayer in the city:

Thought, I love thought,
But not the juggling and twisting of already existent ideas.
I despise that self-important game.
Thought is the welling up of unknown life into conscious-
ness,
Thought is the testing of statements on the touchstone of conscience,
Thought is gazing on the face of life and reading what can be read,
Thought is pondering over experience and coming to conclusion,
Thought is not an exercise or a trick or a set of dodges,
Thought is a man in his wholeness, wholly attending.
(From *Last Poems*)

I particularly like the last line – the idea of attention – of exerting all of what we are to the duty of 'wholly attending' in order that we may fulfil our vocation to be Christ to the world. Robert Schreiter describes this stance in terms of 'a sensitivity to context, an extraordinary capacity to listen and an immersion in the Scriptures'.[348] The inherent discipline in this approach entails the need to avoid on the one hand the unjustified separation[349] of spirituality and theology[350] and, on the other, the lure of activism in situations that frequently leave little or no time to read, think or pray. The use of the word 'immersion' in relation to the Scriptures is important here. All of us know how easy it is to give a merely notional assent to this duty as part of our calling to be students of the word of God. And even serious readers of the Bible know of the days when the enterprise may appear repetitive with little by way of genuine encounter or illumination. I want to suggest that real assent entails what F. D. Maurice described as a readiness 'to dig' – to go deeper in our explorations that avoids superficiality and the repetition that so easily becomes the enemy of spiritual passion. This work is best undertaken together with small groups of people – those who have recognized that prayerful reflection is a costly undertaking that is fundamental to urban mission. A measure of discernment will reveal and encourage such individuals with a gift or aptitude for a disciplined spiritual life that sustains the integrity and witness of the wider congregation.

In 1990 I moved from the familiar confines of a busy and well-attended church in a town that still showed some deference to the Church to a diverse and at times volatile city-centre parish that appeared indifferent[351] to institutional Christianity. To borrow a phrase from Max Weber, most seemed religiously 'unmusical'[352] – no longer able or willing to be moved by our melodies. This in itself proved a significant rite of passage. The lack of support structures, apart from a tiny congregation, was another. I also needed to make sense of the welter of voluntary and statutory activity within the parish boundary and the likely trajectory of the city after years of economic decline and geographical marginalization. This was achieved to some extent by the usual procedures of networking, endless meetings and visits to promote confidence and understanding and the prospects of co-operation for the common good. But it was also underpinned by a prior commitment to prayer, study, Scripture and reflection in relation to the local church and its role concerning the wider social and economic issues of the city. It is difficult to convey the original urgency of this task particularly when the congregation was vulnerable, the needs of the parish considerable and the complexity of Hull even more so. But what I can say is that our renewed commitment to service and evangelism acquired greater depth and resonance because it was nourished and sustained from within by the willed contribution of a small group of people whose specific offering was to a disciplined spirituality. The existence of similar groups is documented elsewhere:

It was in 1990 that we decided it was important to employ a theologian, a member of the team whose primary activity was to pray, reflect and think – not on behalf of others or instead of them but in co-operation with them and to contribute to the work of theological reflection within the Christian community in this area.[353]

It is difficult to quantify the outcome of such commitment but in relation to my time in Hull it contributed to the renewal of the local church and heightened awareness of the needs and contradictions of the city. Equally importantly it helped to foster a new confidence and deeper sense of identity in the congregation that looked beyond survival and no longer saw the city as hostile to its concerns. In this respect a conspicuous feature of other local churches was a lack of confidence in relation to the city and its possibilities. A preoccupation with buildings and a fear of the secular domain made a sense of insularity inevitable. Michael Clevenot highlights the short-coming of these communities when he compares them with St Paul's use of *ecclesia* as designating not 'only a gathering but rather the specific practice of these communities articulated at the economic, political and ideological levels as faith, hope and love'.[354] A disciplined spirituality combined with strategic analysis and social practice assisted one local church to renew its contract with the urban and to see beyond the familiar and enervating issues of apathy and indifference. And crucially it contributed to a fresh understanding of marginality.

Marginality is often interpreted as a location of irrelevance or weakness. In recent years a good deal of writing on the sociology of religion has pointed to the privatization of reli-gion and the way it is pushed to the margins of social and economic life.[355] The sacred canopy that historically provided a framework of meaning for society is now held to reflect only different approaches to matters of lifestyle and spirituality and contributes little or nothing to our social roles in a largely autonomous public domain.[356] Leaving aside the weaknesses of the secularization argument that were touched upon earlier in the chapter, I want to suggest in this section that the margin is not necessarily a bad place to be and is potentially a location of strength for urban mission. It can offer a space in which people can recreate themselves and in which religion retains the ability to matter to a locality. In the right circumstances it can help to arrest or reverse church decline and foster civil society. It can also provide a measure of autonomy that makes possible the necessary distance for a Christian critique of the wider culture. Without this principled marginality, urban mission is unlikely to retain any potency as a sign of contradiction to agencies or powers that prove inimical to the common good. A helpful principle to hold on to here is that of *oscillation*: the city deserves our very best as we work and struggle for its welfare yet, paradoxically, for the sake of the city, a certain detachment is also required. So we find ourselves oscillating between different kinds of activity:

> The movement of withdrawal and renunciation is a necessary element in every Christian life, even though it be followed by an equally necessary movement of responsible engagement in cultural tasks. Where this is lacking, Christian faith quickly degenerates into a utilitarian device for the attainment of personal prosperity or public peace; and some imagined idol called by his name takes the place of Jesus Christ the Lord.[357]

The precept is also evident in the gospels. Jesus moves between the poles of activity and disengagement as he travels restlessly on through the towns and cities and then withdraws into solitude and prayer. We too need to feel at home in the desert and the market place, so to speak, and value them as two alternating modes of experience 'each with its own way of thinking and its own validity',[358] and each contributing to the task of securing justice and compassion for all the inhabitants of the city.

If the margin has many possibilities, where is the evidence? A starting point can be seen in the revival of religion among ethnic minorities in the inner city, a revival which, as Michael Northcott indicates, 'has taken place as the mainstream churches have struggled to sustain a remnant of viable inner-city congregations'.[359] He refers to the attested experience of Asians and Afro-Carribeans and the way in which the mobilization of religion and tradition has provided a bulwark against secularization and racism.[360] The power of ethnicity at the margin indicates that even when the pressures towards secularization are conceded they encounter resistance at the local level where there is space for distinctive forms of religious life to flourish.

Flourishing takes place on the margin but, crucially, it is not confined there. Ethnic religious practice with its endearing love of exuberant prayer and praise, frequently spills over into concerted action[361] in the city to counter racism, violence and injustice. It is a practice worthy of emulation and it is not beyond the imagination of urban churches to adopt an *interpretation of the margin* that endorses it as a place that can make a difference to the surrounding culture. This will not just be a matter of faith and hope or even the readiness to learn from the experience of non-Christian communities. It has to do instead with the acceptance that time and place do matter in the general scheme of things and the belief that the local is to be valued as a source of power with a freedom to shape affairs otherwise. A surfeit of disappointment or failure on the part of urban practitioners can easily vitiate any sense of this rich potential at the margin but there are encouraging examples that reveal it as a hospitable place where individuals and communities can change their lives. Margaret Walsh's account of how a community group in Wolverhampton brought about the relocation of a poisonous battery recycling plant shows what can be achieved.[362]

On this reading of the margin, the urban future is not a closed book for the Church. There are dangers and risks but as the next chapter will show, there are also opportunities and alliances to be made that call into question the theological pessimism of an earlier time. It is simply false, as Harvey Cox once avowed, that the Church has no power to heal in the city[363] and can only be a passive recipient of whatever forces are loosed upon it. The power to do otherwise, however, is bound up with how we see the margin – as both a familiar element of a locality and a venue for the indwelling of God. As John Robinson once remarked, 'truth is two eyed':[364] in the crucible of the urban a particular kind of vision is required that registers and responds to the hurts and vulnerabilities of deprived communities yet is still able to find delight and wonder in the sacraments of God's presence – 'hospitals, shops, sewers and dustbin collection all gifts in their fascinating complexity'.[365] To see the city in this transfigured light also calls for a perceptive trust that is open and hospitable to the *quiddity*[366] of things and their inner savour.

Complex issues are entailed here. The suggestion is that the margin opens up the possibility of encounter with the gracious source of all things, God. Yet divine grace does not coerce, does not insist that there should always be a transforming engagement. We are free not to receive, not to trust, not to recognize that a local church as 'a serious house on serious earth'[367] should always show respect to the ordinary and commonplace as the handiwork and habitation of God. The liberating power of the margin therefore is constrained or released by the refusal or reception that is accorded to it by the household of faith. Everything depends on tact, courtesy of mind, a capacity for welcome or denial and a subtle recognition that it takes 'two freedoms to make one'[368] when 'face to face with the presence of offered meaning'.[369]

Despite labouring over these words, I know that in a world that sometimes appears metaphysically tone deaf they will appear strange, odd, ridiculous even. Yet for me they represent no particular difficulty and point, however inadequately, to the sacramental reality of God that is to be found through a patient attention to common things. It is a matter of seeing and listening, of cleansing our perceptions and awareness in order that the energies of God may be discerned in the minute particulars of the margin that are shot through with mystery and offer unexpected disclosures. Jon McGregor's recent debut novel is set on a street in a North of England town. He writes about ordinary people doing normal things and the shabby and melancholy contexts that form the backcloth of their lives. But with his opening lines he alerts us to the continuing wonder of the city and its hidden meanings:

> If you listen, you can hear it.
> The city, it sings.
> If you stand quietly, at the foot of a garden, in the middle of a street, on the roof of a house.
> It's clearest at night, when the sound cuts more sharply across the surface of things, when the song reaches out to a place inside you.
> It's a wordless song, for the most, but it's a song all the same, and nobody hearing it could doubt what it sings.
> And the song sings the loudest when you pick out each note.[370]

The city sings – its disparate sounds 'all come together and rouse like a choir'[371] in praise of the present moment, its claim on our attention and the necessity, on our part, of a poetic response. In an 'Essay on Poetry' in 1829, Newman commented that 'With Christians a poetical view of things is a duty.'[372] Poets have often told us that we live in an enchanted world where the infinite is to be found in everything, and at the heart of the gospel – always tantalizingly a footstep away – stands the poet from Nazareth, the true Son of God singing his songs and beckoning us to share in life's wonder and sadness. Yet the churches have not always made the connection between poetry, prayer and vision. Equally, beauty and truth will often go unrecognized unless our way of looking is informed by the poetic – the awakening within ourselves to the mysterious continuum we call the present and the invitation to a deeper engagement with God through an attitude of attentive waiting.[373] These are strenuous commands yet the invitation to pray, look and see is not always declined. The following verses formed part of a service commemorating the work of the Church Urban Fund on Merseyside:

I saw a vision:
it was last Thursday at eleven o'clock in the morning.
I was standing at the top of Ashurst Beacon, looking down
over the towns of this Lancashire plain, and out to sea
when the cold, blue autumn sky broke over my head
and the Spirit of God breathed on my eyes and my eyes were
opened:
I saw Liverpool, the holy city, coming down out of heaven
shining like a rare jewel, sparkling like clear water in the eye
of the sun
and all the sickness was gone from the city
and there were no more suburbs and schemes
no difference between Hightown and Huyton
I saw the Mersey running with the water of life,
as bright as crystal,
as clear as glass
the children of Liverpool swimming in it.
I saw an old woman throw back her head
and laugh like a young girl
and when the sky closed back her laughter rang in my head
for days and days
and would not go away.
This is what I saw, looking across this northern English
landscape,
looking up from the city of death
and I knew then that there would be a day of resurrection
and I believe that there will be a day of resurrecton.[374]

In this chapter I have outlined the theological principles that
are now required to shape, sustain and direct the work of local
urban churches as they seek to embody the love of God in a
disciplined, reflective and imaginative way. Taken together,
the principles represent a way of doing theology – of theology
as a method, a way of looking at things, a standpoint or
perspective informed by prayer, silence and study. Implied in
all these activities is the notion of theology as a practical
undertaking grounded in Scripture and doctrine but validated

by specific acts and practices. Theology lacks coherence without the beliefs and formulations that constitute its distinctive grammar but it perishes unless these same articles of faith are authenticated by outward and visible signs – 'by their fruits shall ye know them' (Matt. 7.20). In the remaining pages I want to suggest the ways in which Christian communities can fulfil their vocation as the people of God in our global urban society.

6 'A Broad and Living Way':
Doing Love's Work

As a philosopher, Immanuel Kant always had three questions at the back of his mind: what can we know, what may we hope and what ought we to do? We know a considerable amount about the twenty-first-century city with its power to inspire and fascinate and, as we have seen, much is being written about the future of urban society from a global perspective. I have also suggested that when theology and prayer combine to spark imaginative thinking we may genuinely hope and work for the renewal of urban communities. Time and place are never bereft of opportunity or possibility and, as Walter Wink notes, 'History belongs to the intercessors who believe the future into being.'[375] But what ought we to *do* in the city as we pray and reflect and seek to understand its complex processes? The question matters for two reasons. First, urban mission is fuelled by a wide range of dynamics and the city represents diverse meanings. No two congregations share exactly the same agenda; no two clergy will be driven by identical dreams, hopes, theological presuppositions and expectations. A broad range of religious ideas and insights inspired the admirable women and men of the nineteenth century who resolved that the poor should not be forgotten in the burgeoning towns and cities. More than a century later it is evident that this same kind of theological untidiness persists.[376] Urban mission is a 'tangle of complexities' and local congregations need to embrace a model of witness that fits the particularities of their context.[377] Second, against a backcloth of falling clergy numbers, frozen budgets and finance-driven policies, questions are bound to be raised concerning the extent to which urban ministry continues to represent a good return on investment. Minds bent on cost-effectiveness might well be tempted to transfer or regroup scarce resources when inner-city congregations have little to show by way of conspicuous achievements – that is, financial and numerical growth. What are we to do in difficult situations that frequently elude the predictable parameters of success yet require the unstinting offering of the local church?

I am not about to duck this question but I do want to make some preliminary remarks before advancing four specific proposals. Although I shall try to present these in a reasonably clear form they do not amount to a mini-manual for urban mission. Experience and research alike point to the fact that the surging life of the city is always moving on in ways that cannot easily be predicted or recorded. Its needs and the responses demanded from us can never be satisfactorily fixed in a handbook. A proper element of provisionality needs to inform our thinking and practice and a readiness to begin again without too much regret or disappointment when plans or initiatives fail. Staying in the city requires patience and a readiness to take the long view – pleasure when things go well and a refusal to mope when desired outcomes are thwarted. It's a form of Christian stoicism without succumbing to the temptation of falling on our swords if matters become unbelievably bad. Prayer and laughter can help us here.

A quotation that I occasionally use at clergy gatherings has its origins in an ordination address given by a former bishop of Oxford. As his clergy trembled on the brink of uncharted waters he said to them, 'Develop a sense of humour and live on your knees.' I like its pithiness and have found it to be a serviceable maxim over the years. Living on our knees is about the centrality of prayer amid the confusions of the city, of not losing the desire for this daily task and the readiness to embrace, where possible with others, a disciplined spirituality.

What I am referring to here is not just depth but persistence – not how we ought to pray but the preparedness to carry on with the business of silence and intercession because it represents the heart of the matter:

> To pray is to place oneself in the silent presence of the Eternal Beyond, the God of Truth and Love, and letting the flow of communication between that and one's truest self clarify the distorted vision, purify the motives, countervail the pressures and set one free from dependence upon any other power except the care for others which holds on, trusting, hoping and enduring, until in the long term it wins through.[378]

We know these sentiments to be true but it is persistence – 'trusting, hoping and enduring' – and the humility which recognizes that prayer demands the best of us, that set these truths as a seal upon our hearts. Laughter, in contrast, stops us from taking ourselves too seriously – not least in relation to the practice of prayer where the gap between aspiration and performance will sometimes be comical. The city is no place for the po-faced or excessively pious. It is the testing ground *par excellence* of both the veracity of our truth claims and the measure of our humanity, our readiness to smile when life is frequently incongruous, unfair or odd. The city is in turn a carnival, a riot, a theatre of nascent dreams, a sanctuary and an asylum. A place of strange meetings, unexpected encounters, deep poignancy and even deeper sorrows. Even to begin to describe the city in this way is to open the floodgate of memory: the parish carol-singing group that included an arsonist, a murderer and a teacher of classics among its number; the neighbour from the mental health 'safe' house who kicked down our garden shed and later (by way of apology perhaps?) took the poppy appeal collection box to the British Legion only to have second thoughts on the way and decided to buy a bike with the proceeds instead. The young man pushing his hands through the letter box after midnight asking me to bless them for he was afraid; the older man kneeling at the doorstep, naked to the waist and covered entirely from head to navel in brown boot polish. The peculiar ritual of New Year's Eve when stepping soberly (and somewhat diffidently) across the threshold of the local pub on the stroke of midnight, I would in turn become confidant and entertainer – one minute learning the secrets of the human heart and the next thrust on to a makeshift stage to perform some impromptu karaoke. The alcoholic who, thwarted by not being able to kick down our front door, would opt for screaming to the whole estate what a lying, cheating cleric I was and then, next morning, having completely forgotten the incidents of the previous night, would ask to clean the vicarage windows. The brothers on the road needing a bath, shave, food and clothing; both pleasant enough if somewhat reticent which, as it later transpired, may have had something to do with the police pursuing them in connection with the theft of a corpse. And finally, for our purposes here and possibly out of his desire not to be outdone, I must acknowledge the other young man on the road who, unamused by my effort to be cheerful, threw a bottle of scalding tea over me before moving on to Derby in an attempt to burn down its cathedral.

The comic and the tragic form part of the heartbeat of urban life. Laughter and a sense of humour afford us a perspective on the pageant and remind us that we are all passing through, strangers and pilgrims, but ultimately, by divine grace, invited guests at the wedding feast of the Lamb. The heavenly banquet is part of the promise contained in the book of Revelation to all those who love God. And laughter is a foretaste of that redeemed time when the promise will be fulfilled.[379]

But, to return to the original question, what of this time and the urban life that confronts us now? What is our business in the city and is there a controlling image to describe what we should be doing? As we have seen from the earlier survey of urban mission there are various roles available to the Christian community ranging from revolutionary to more traditional ways of being Church. A helpful picture for me is that of the *bricoleur*. Claude Lévi-Strauss describes the *bricoleur* as the person who makes do with what is at hand – the tools, materials and resources that are available, the inherited bits and pieces that we choose to retain on the basis of their continuing utility.[380] I am intrigued by the image and, as I see it, the process of *bricolage* has relevance for the work of urban mission. The *bricoleur* takes stock of the problems that need addressing and the resources available for solving them. Then she proceeds creatively (and with an element of provisionality that reflects the tenuous nature of the city) by 'putting together, reordering, weighting, weeding out and filling in'.[381] This is not system building or the work, say, of an engineer. It is more tentative, open to the imagination and the resources of the past and responsive to current challenges. And it does seem to chime with the arguments, suggestions and overall approach that are being advocated here. So – to delay no longer – let me advance the four discrete elements, the serviceable bits and pieces that corroborate the reformulated theology of the previous chapter.

In the first instance, I want to say something about the significance of corporate worship for Christian identity and the ways in which liturgy and ritual are able to address social dis-ease and exclusion. Worship is the secret weapon of the Church and, as Temple observed, is the means whereby we try to save the world. A second argument will emphasize the contribution of local churches to the promotion of civil society through the provision of space that fosters civility, trust and a sense of common purpose. Third, I shall argue that a concomitant of promoting civil society will entail 'the intentional and strategic commitment'[382] of urban churches to partnerships that can help reverse economic and social decline. In view of the rejection and personal despair experienced by many in the inner city, a case will also be made for the continuing necessity of what one great nineteenth-century social reformer described as 'this deep, difficult, holy work'[383] – unstinting care and compassion for the individual.

Worship, Identity and Mission

In Chapter 2, I referred to the paucity of material in *Faith in the City* in relation to the social nature of liturgy and the extent to which it calls worshippers to a costly involvement in the life of the world. The Archbishop's Commission described worship as a means of fostering good dreams in the harsh reality of UPAs and drew attention to its importance as a means of evangelism through its power to evoke the presence of God.[384] But what is lacking in its description of liturgy is any powerful sense of worship as a focus for Christian identity and community and a 'regulative principle of all our theology and all our work'.[385] Let me then give two reasons to support the claim that the building up of a worshipping community is crucial to the future of the urban church.

Christian Identity and Formation

A coherent and cohesive sense of Christian identity becomes more not less important in contexts where we are all now cosmopolitan citizens and the local can no longer be defined purely in territorial or geographical terms. Yet in an illuminating discussion of the place of worship in UPAs and its contribution to Christian nurture, Ford and McFadyen note the striking fact that 'a great deal of Christian discussion, analysis and activity in these areas seems to have little or no living relation to the basic Christian activity of worship'.[386] Corroboration of this claim can be found in the progress reports on *Faith in the City* neither of which devote any serious attention to liturgical worship and its relation to urban mission or its significance for diocesan strategies.[387] This diffidence or neglect is further compounded by the presumed agnosticism of the wider culture:

> Newspapers, television, our educational system and the rest of our culture deeply condition us to an agnostic or atheist 'realism'. This becomes normality, an orthodoxy which

labels anyone taking God seriously as odd, or at best holding curious private beliefs of no public importance. The conditions of UPAs (at least as commonly understood) often lend themselves to reinforcing this. Christians in UPAs are in the grip of this false normality as much as any others. For those most concerned about the conditions, there is also the special danger of an activist, problem-solving realism which loses the life of praise and leaves them wondering what the significance of their faith in God is in relation to their commitments and the whole situation.[388]

Personally (and for reasons alluded to in the previous chapter), I am not quite so pessimistic in my reading of modern times and the mass media but I do recognize from my own experience and that of others working in the city that to lose the life of praise is to fall prey to exhaustion and disorientation. Furthermore, in a culture that is not disposed to acknowledge God as the horizon within which everything else happens, a significant shift is required in our thought and imagination if a distinctive religious and ethical vision is to be sustained, a shift which recognizes that 'we see the truth and possibilities of each other most adequately when we are most fully taken up with God'[389] and that worship is the medium which gives memory, meaning and identity to local congregations. Paradoxically, for all the stress on action as the key to the role of the urban Church since *Faith in the City* there now needs to be an equally strong emphasis on worship as an integrated and natural outworking of a disciplined spirituality.

A measure of clarity will also be useful in relation to the nature and purpose of worship for the issues at stake touch our self-understanding concerning what we are *for* in the city as, alongside others, we try to build the new Jerusalem, 'the well-founded city, designed and built by God' (Heb. 11.10). The point of worship is to direct us to God: at its heart is praise expressed so emphatically in the opening words of the 'Te Deum': 'You are God and we praise you; you are the Lord and we acclaim you.' Worship derives its power from adoration, its acknowledgement of transcendence and its recognition of the local congregation as both a fellowship and 'the earthly heaven in which the heavenly God dwells and moves'.[390] Only when a Christian community is caught up with something bigger than just its own needs and concerns can we begin to talk of liturgy as an exercise in self-forgetfulness. G. K. Chesterton once helpfully pointed out in this respect that the reason angels can fly is because they think lightly of themselves.

Apart from the invitation to get ourselves off our hands a little, liturgy also calls us back to our roots and the realization that from its beginnings the household of faith has worshipped. The Acts of the Apostles and the letters of Paul bear witness to the fact that common prayer as a shared activity of the gathered congregation is a practice which has its roots in the earliest period of the Church. A century later Justin Martyr describes the assembly of worshipping Christians:

> And on the day called Sunday, all who live in cities or in the country gather together to one place, and the memoirs of the apostles or the writings of the prophets are read, as long as time permits; then, when the reader has ceased, the president verbally instructs, and exhorts to the imitation of these good things. Then we all rise together and pray, and, as we before said, when our prayer is ended, bread and wine and water are brought, and the president in like manner offers prayers and thanksgivings, according to his ability, and the people assent, saying Amen.[391]

The scene is outwardly unremarkable yet we know that, when oppression and persecution afflicted the Church, members of such gatherings were prepared to be tortured and executed rather than cease participating in these rites. How are we to account for their resistance even on pain of death and, no less significantly, the continuing readiness of congregations to worship so many generations later? Karl Barth is intrigued by the question and he sees that part of the answer is bound up with the mystery of God in Christ and the strange instinct that brings worshippers to the edge of things they barely understand in a 'building old or new . . . that is thought of as a place of extraordinary doings'.[392] Describing the liturgical leadership of the local minister he goes on to say:

> And then the man will have the congregation sing ancient songs full of weird and weighty memories, strange ghostly witnesses of the sufferings, struggles, and triumphs of the long-departed fathers, all leading to the edge of an immeasurable event, all, whether the minister and people understand what they are singing or not, full of reminiscences of God, always of God. 'God is present! God *is* present.'[393]

Note the italic and the tense: God *is* present. In this gathering worshippers are reshaped. Their local story intersects with the universal Christian story and 'in turn corporate memory and identity are refreshed'.[394] Through the offering of prayer and praise and particularly in the celebration of the Eucharist, the local congregation by participating in Christ not only discovers its role of belonging within the long history of the wider Church but is also brought to the realization that its mission can never be abstracted from the world. As Bonhoeffer notes: 'Sharing in Christ we stand at once in both the reality of God and the reality of the world. The reality of Christ comprises the reality of the world within itself.'[395] To understand and indwell this claim requires more than intelligence. It demands from some, as I argued in the previous chapter a disciplined spirituality, and from everyone the recognition that in religious terms ultimate reality is mediated 'not just in the world of the . . . understanding, but concretely through the forming of a community'.[396] For this reason a renewed stress needs to be placed on worship 'for worship enables the church to *become* a divine community, a visible testimony to the world . . . while also working at healthy integration with, and service[397] of the locality in which it is placed'.[398]

Two further comments. The previous paragraphs should

not be seen as an argument for elevating worship over and above any other activity of the local congregation; that, in other words, worship should be offered for worship's sake without any other consideration or end. They point instead, and in so doing corroborate my experience in Hull and Merseyside, to the symbiotic and crucial relationship between worship, identity and social action. If, as Kenneth Leech asserts, the primary theological task is praise and prayer[399] this is because such activities lead not only to the contemplation and adoration of God but also to the transformation and redemption of local communities.

It may be argued that the links being made here between worship, identity and responsible service bear little resemblance to the vapid or boring liturgies that are frequently a visible feature of congregational life where there is little by way of celebration or expectation and everything appears leaden or perfunctory. I want to say therefore that enlivening worship is still to be found in the city. Moderately catholic liturgies in Hull replete with vestments, bells and incense were characterized by diversity, mutuality and a preparedness to be a 'burden bearer'[400] for others while still retaining a strong sense of identity. In his most recent book on urban ministry, Laurie Green provides a moving example of how a local act of worship was able to embrace human distress in an immediate and tangible way:

> Sitting in St Peter's church one evening, my attention was drawn to a young man who sat on a chair amid a group of other youngsters. As the service progressed I began to realize that he was suffering from Tourette Syndrome, that acute mental illness which prompts one to shout obscenities uncontrollably. From time to time the young man would lose control, swear very loudly, and then slap his own face in self-recrimination. I saw a young woman in the group lean over and put her arm consolingly around him to comfort him in his distress and shame, and to assure him that his presence was welcomed and his problem understood by the

other young worshippers. I would have thought that the intrusion of such extreme obscenities in the midst of worship would have marred the whole occasion, and yet on the contrary, it became for us all a very significant mark of God's compassion in the midst of profound suffering.[401]

Elsewhere, Ford and McFadyen have also gathered accounts of the catholicity of urban worship that indicate 'a strikingly strong stream of testimonies from UPAs'[402] that point to the transforming power of liturgy for the way life is lived in and beyond the Christian community:

> At its heart is the crucified God, the gathering around the body broken for the world. People can bring their whole selves to be fed and transformed – which means the whole of their situations, their sins, their joys and griefs, hopes and fears, tragedies and successes, the groups and institutions which help structure their world.[403]

To these stories and testimonies we can also add important findings from recent social science research[404] that show the positive influence of regular liturgical worship on the attitudes of congregations to the wider community. Robin Gill has noted, for example, that the singing of hymns is itself an act of formation that leads to lives being reordered under God through a renewed commitment to the wider environment.[405] It seems that we can become what we sing, carriers and interpreters in a most practical way of the truths and doctrines enshrined in our hymnals and liturgies – sacraments on legs and Christ to others.

Imagination and Mission

Another fruit of transforming worship is that of a developed imagination. Just as a poetic sensibility enables us to see the council estate and the high street as more than marginal and mundane facts, imagination is also able to identify the underlying significance of things in the world.[406] In this sense it is normally taken to describe the work of the creative artist but it is no less applicable to the praise, prayer and adoration of worship that enable reality to be imagined differently:

> Our way of imagining ourselves and others is (often very slowly and precariously) transformed by the amazed recognition of our dignity and theirs before God. God's way of giving us dignity does not just mean our being passive receivers. It can also excite us to all sorts of overflowing generative activity.[407]

The claim reflects the experiences of the authors and many like them who have spent years living and worshipping in the inner city. The fusion of worship and imagination allows the future to be 'praised open'.[408] It helps to bring about a different perspective on how things appear including those that contradict the will of God and a renewed commitment to a different future for impoverished localities. Liturgy is therefore a social act, rooted in rites and ceremonies that can quicken the spirit and induce 'an extraordinary power of redescribing reality'.[409] And none of this is magic. Liturgy feeds the imagination precisely because it draws its symbolism from the cycles and transitions we experience in human life and invites our willed attention on a crucified, resurrected and ascended Christ, on his broken and resplendent body as a prefiguring of community as it could be:

> In the resurrection and ascension of Christ can be seen the blurring, the overlap of God's place and humanity's – we glimpse this locality transfused and transfigured by the next. This is the staggering confession of the Church, that because of this little, local, life, death and resurrection, *all* little, local life might be changed.[410]

The important thing to grasp here is that this huge doctrinal claim, centred on the power of Christ to become a compelling point of reference for the missionary task, depends on the power of liturgy to remind us of our religious origins while enabling us to sing a new song that speaks of a promised world in the making, even in the midst of disorder and chaos. We look back and drink from our own wells and, looking towards the city, glimpse it as a 'human awful wonder of God'[411] where heaven is already inaugurated. Liturgy becomes life giving, a moment of liberation for the imagination. Far from being unproductive or, frankly, a waste of time, liturgy challenges us to worship God alone and to work for the city which has still to be made. To engage in this task and to bring to it our deepest longing for the peaceable kingdom of which the prophets and Jesus spoke is to take the first step in the remaking of local communities. Worship is infinitely worthwhile.

Remaking Civil Society

Before introducing my second argument, a little bit of transatlantic background will be helpful. In 1995 the Harvard political scientist Robert Putnam made an important observation. Noting that more Americans were taking up ten pin bowling than before, but fewer were becoming members of leagues, he called it 'bowling alone'.[412] Drawing on this insight he went on to describe how the social fabric of communities was in decline: there was less neighbourliness about, fewer people were joining voluntary groups, the young were disaffected with politics. Important 'habits of association'[413] were being eroded and in consequence people were becoming more suspicious of others, less trusting and therefore less inclined to have confidence in authorities and institutions. Civil society was under threat.[414]

The debate has extended to our own shores in recent years. In 2002 the annual BBC Reith lectures were given by the philosopher, Onora O'Neill, who over five weeks examined the nature of trust, its role in society and everyday life and the extent to which there was evidence of a crisis of trust. She began with an insight from Confucius that she still found convincing. He told his disciple Tsze-kung that three things were needed for government: weapons, food and trust. If a ruler cannot hold on to all three, he should give up the weapons first and the food next. Trust should be guarded to the end for 'without trust we cannot stand'.[415] It lies at the core of much of our personal and civic lives and, for O'Neill, a wise government will persuade its citizens not simply to behave in particular ways but to invest in and help create a culture of trustworthiness.

It may therefore be more than coincidence that the present (2003) Labour administration has highlighted the need to improve the fabric of society in the most disadvantaged areas and has readily acknowledged the role of urban churches as a vital source of care and insights in the building up of trust and common purposes. In a R. H. Tawney Lecture, Stephen Timms MP affirmed that 'we need church and church-based projects working with us . . . churches have people, energy, commitment, local knowledge and buildings that are key assets'.[416] The Home Secretary, David Blunkett, has also called on faith communities to assist the Government in this task of renewal. Speaking at a celebration to mark the diamond jubilee of the Churches Main Committee (CMC), an ecumenical agency set up to co-operate with government in the development of public policy, he commented:

> Every faith has a development worker, full or part-time, paid or voluntary: in other words, the priest or pastor, the vicar or minister, the teacher, imam or rabbi. This is a resource available to all areas of our country, even the most deprived, the least active and the most likely to be disengaged from the political process. This is a resource that even government regeneration programmes and the development of community leadership cannot match.[417]

There is an implicit recognition in both remarks that the intangible qualities of trust, reciprocity, mutual obligation and duty towards the community are essential to any meaningful notion of citizenship and the wider stability and prosperity of society. The State depends on virtues that cannot be created by programmes or policies alone. Social capital – the glue that holds communities together – is a precious commodity that cannot be generated by financial institutions and exists beyond the corridors of power. The welfare of the city depends upon it. T. S. Eliot recognized this. It is worth recalling as we read the following lines that Eliot's poetry cannot be divorced from the nine years he spent working in a major London bank:

> When the Stranger says: 'What is the meaning of this city?
> Do you huddle close together because you love each other?'
> What will you answer? 'We all dwell together
> To make money from each other?' or 'This is a community?'
> And the Stranger will depart and return to the desert.
> O my soul, be prepared for the coming of the Stranger,
> Be prepared for him who knows how to ask questions.[418]

The Stranger coming to the city today still intent on asking questions would presumably wish to know *where* the virtues are created that enable and encourage individuals to help one another without coercion or the prospect of gain. The answer is to be found at the local – the voluntary associations, communities and fellowships of various kinds – religious or otherwise. Edmund Burke, we recall, famously described these modest but crucially important organizations as 'little platoons' that give rise to 'public affections'.[419] Despite the massive changes in post-war Britain since 1945 accompanied by a decline in more traditional groupings, new local organizations continue to emerge committed to a variety of concerns ranging from self-help to care of the environment.[420] They point to the continuing strength of small but useful enterprises that bring grace and civility to our common life and nurture our sense of belonging.[421] Urban churches, particularly in terms of their identity as faith communities, are well placed to make a useful contribution to this task of renewing civil society as will be seen from the personal stories in the following section.

Church Buildings

The Church in the inner town, and on the large overspill estate, can easily be caught in a poverty trap. Its impossible burdens of fabric and finance can kill its missionary morale, and thus the life of the local church gets progressively both weaker and more inward looking.

The above remark represents part of a diocesan submission recorded in *Faith in the City* as it addressed the 'serious and complex'[422] question of church buildings. They also convey familiar sentiments in any discussion of urban mission and sometimes lead to the assumption that church buildings are no more than disposable plant that presage the need for new and more imaginative ways of being a local church:

The local church . . . might abandon its sacred buildings . . . setting up house fellowships, opening an office or shop front in the high street with professional staff on hand to deal with a range of religious and social needs, and working in close co-operation with social services, medical practices and schools . . . All this would be meant to equip the Church to respond to the secular sphere rather than acting as a sanctuary set over against it.[423]

Utility marks this model along with a commendable effort at partnership. In certain contexts, the inexorable decay of a building or the movement and change of surrounding population may constitute the only viable way for a congregation to retain a presence in a neighbourhood.[424] But the losses of this model need to be acknowledged too. Distinctiveness matters for a local church. It is not just that a church building enables us to see down the throat of time or makes sense of our destinies in stone. It has to do with the basic and immensely useful fact that when a local church chooses to interact with and serve its parish it starts with a considerable asset in its premises:

The possession of plant equips every church with a specific means of serving the parish. Parishioners are able to come on their own initiative to use whatever the church provides. This may be a simple service such as giving help in writing a letter or filling in a form. It might be giving food to home-less callers, providing a warm room where tea is available, or holding a jumble sale. It is normal to think of church plant as a drain on resources, but in a UPA all premises are themselves a crucial resource.[425]

Pastoral care is the main concern here but there is another facet of church buildings that also has enormous relevance for the promotion of civil society. Churches remain the largest voluntary association in the nation and their buildings make possible assembly, conversation, public discussion and forum for dialogue. All these things promote people's participation in society both at the local level and increasingly in wider contexts in view of the convergence of global forces within localities. Within these frameworks civil society is able to provide a voice for those who are frequently excluded from debate or decision making, 'a valued independence from political parties and business interests'[426] and an opportunity for education as individuals gather to share new insights and concerns and the ability to respond to them. It is in this connection that Shanks notes that 'the quality of public ethical debate seems to be at its best where civil society in general happens to be strongest'.[427] Often in situations where there is a serious need to promote such exchanges, for example, engaging with regeneration programmes, a local UPA church can have a significance far beyond anything which a count of committed members might indicate:

It is hugely significant that, in areas where the motive for assembly on a public issue is most often protest, there are regular assemblies of people meeting together to praise God, to celebrate the common life and to be of service to one another and to neighbours. There are places where these assemblies offer some of the very few opportunities for people with radically dissimilar life histories and attitudes to meet one another in circumstances where mutual understanding can be deepened.[428]

Beyond the provision of structures and locations that enable individuals to retain and enhance a measure of responsibility for ordering their affairs, church buildings can also mobilize and assemble the creativity and talents of a community that shape its welfare and future. Ideas may fall stillborn within a locality until a UPA church acts as a catalyst to bring individuals and agencies together.

In 1999 as vicar of a town-centre UPA parish in Southport, Merseyside, I met with the local Council for Voluntary Service to discuss the provision of a Sunday morning service that would celebrate the contributions of voluntary workers who in their varied roles were offering care in the community. A church event of this kind had not taken place in the remembered past but the CVS Co-ordinator was enthusiastic and invitations with an explanatory letter were distributed. The response was encouraging, particularly from smaller organizations. On Sunday, 18 July 1999, in the presence of the Bishop of Liverpool as the Guest Speaker, a congregation of almost 500 assembled representing more than 70 local agencies. The service proved a spirited occasion that affirmed the work and worth of those present and enabled them afterwards to meet with each other in a way that would not normally have been possible because the sectors they represented were a mystery to each other:

> Partnerships may be the word at the moment but there is precious little evidence of it resulting in intelligent connections. Recently I spent some months looking at how South London worked . . . There was no shortage of initiatives . . . but many were working in isolation . . . And the real experts in making cities better places to live – the city dwellers – were not in the debate.[429]

The service in Southport responded to this challenge by bringing together under one roof different agencies and individuals that ostensibly shared a common purpose, were therefore partners, yet largely worked independently of each other most of the time. No less significantly, the provision of a church building, highly visible as a house of God, fostered communal solidarity and trust that in a modest but important way enabled a range of intermediate associations from services to critical pressure groups to feel their collective strength as significant participants in local civil society. In drawing others into an experience of grace, the building also provided in a literal sense a concrete space in which people momentarily entered and experienced the connections that existed between them. In retrospect it is hard, if not impossible to envisage how all this might have been facilitated in the absence of a visible church or how any other secular institution might have succeeded in bringing a diverse body of people together for such an occasion. The building and the service made a distinctive contribution to civil society by meeting a local need for celebration, ritual and symbol and interpreting a wide range of religious experience.[430]

Sanctuary and Community

A church building has a further contribution to make in the form of a tangible sanctuary, a secure space and place that makes possible the healing of pain and the sustaining of hope and community in situations that frequently threaten both enterprises. It can be a therapeutic centre where memories can be healed, wounds tended and trust nurtured. The task of civil society at one level is about rebuilding fragmented lives and a local UPA church can create the atmosphere which makes this possible. Two personal stories come immediately to mind.

In the early 1990s, I organized a Maundy Thursday church vigil. Shortly after midnight there was a persistent knocking at the church door: a man from the adjacent council estate came in. His wife had recently died and the initial stage of grief was leaving him overwhelmed and confused. He was not a member of the congregation but the church had organized her funeral service. He asked if he could sit alone in front of the imposing crucifix that dominated the sanctuary and altar and conveyed in an awsome way the suffering of Christ. For 30 minutes he talked audibly to his deceased partner and then left quietly.

During one week of the summer of 2001 three young people, two male, one female, came into my church in Southport to sit quietly either in the side chapel or the nave. Initially there was no request for help or counsel: the only requirement was to be offered a space for reflection and prayer. Before leaving they did disclose something of their backgrounds and it transpired that in each case they had been the victim of abuse in relation to parent or partner. The need for redemptive space constituted part of the continuing work of healing and acceptance.

By offering sanctuary each UPA church was able to contribute to the restoration of damaged humanity. As places committed to a Christ-like God and the unceasing work of human reconciliation, they took seriously the religious obligation to assist the lost souls who entered their doors. It is not to claim too much that in seeking sanctuary these individuals were looking for a way to place their story of hurt, injustice and loss inside the narrative of Christ's Passion.[431] That they came to a church building also suggests that amid the diversity and discordances of the urban a local church is still able to provide a language and a space[432] along with an atmosphere of trust that contributes to civil society.

Partnerships at Work

In this section I am going to draw on my parish experience in Hull to show how partnerships were embraced to the mutual benefit of the church and the local community. A local congregation renewed itself and was able to sustain its mission alongside the poor and powerless.[433]

St Paul's, Hull

Part of my decision to minister for five years in the centre of Hull from 1990 to 1995 was to test a hypothesis, the feasibility of a very small congregation achieving numerical growth and also making a quantifiable difference to an area characterized by acute social deprivation and a long-standing indifference, sometimes bordering on hostility, to organized religion. Initially the congregation numbered eight people, including two churchwardens. A long interregnum preceded by a short tenure on the part of the previous priest-in-charge had created a climate of uncertainty and introversion in the congregation; scant financial and human resources precluded the possibility of any missionary strategy to the city or the adjoining council estate. The shape of the building, erected in 1979 following the demolition of a much earlier church on an adjacent site, did not identify it as a church and it was not uncommon to discover that some residents on the estate thought it was a community centre where they went to vote at local elections. At night the building was completely invisible, dwarfed by surrounding factories. An early decision was taken to install an illuminated cross outside the building. Although the cross was occasionally vandalized it proved a positive innovation that brought a distinctive identity to the church and, to a surprising degree, encouragement to some beyond the congregation. Neighbours telephoned local radio to express their delight and one driver even made a special point of seeing the cross on her way home: 'It picks me up after a bad day caring for the severely mentally ill' was the reason she gave for her occasional detour.

The parish population, entirely working class, was approximately four thousand, incorporating a council estate and a third of the city centre. A very significant feature of the parish was the large number of statutory and voluntary agencies concentrated within its boundaries. The statutory included the Fire Brigade, Police Headquarters, Ambulance Service and Social Services Headquarters. In addition there were voluntary agencies working with the elderly, homeless, drug addicts, AIDS/HIV sufferers, youth, the unemployed and individuals with mental health problems. There was also a State Primary School and a Roman Catholic Primary School. I made reference in the previous chapter to the decision to engage with these various agencies as part of an initial networking procedure and the desire to promote trust and the possibilities of partnership. Underpinning this approach was the realization that the local church had to grow numerically to avoid continuing decline and, also, no less importantly, to become an effective partner in community regeneration. Door-to-door visiting on the estate was complemented by meetings with local agencies to discuss, plan and eventually initiate a range of projects designed to meet specific social and economic needs. The projects included the following.

- A Sunday Club run in conjunction with MIND for people with mental health problems. This provided leisure and educational amenities along with counselling facilities. Up to 50 people were able to assemble in a relaxed and welcoming atmosphere. Previously there had been no provision of this sort over the weekend as statutory agencies and centres were closed. The local church was uniquely placed to shore up this gap in service provision.
- A centre for the unemployed on the council estate to boost morale and improve job opportunities. This was run in conjunction with the local Community Association and initially grant-aided by CUF. The relationship with the Community Association eventually led to short, informal Sunday afternoon services being held in the centre.
- A weekly Monday evening 'Travellers' Club' for children up to the age of 13 organized by the church with assistance provided by local social services and the Diocesan Children's Officer. A varied programme of activities was implemented using the church rooms as a base but incorporating regular social outings. The need for this facility was particularly acute on a council estate where a secure place in which

children could play was virtually non-existent, being confined to a recreational ground that had effectively been
appropriated by drug users and gangs. Concerning the
duty and responsibility of the UPA church in this respect
Northcott comments:

> The Church, locally and nationally, should also be active
> in pressing, lobbying and organizing for children to find a
> safe space, a wild place, in which to play, for in children's
> play are repeated the timeless and culture-transcending
> themes of the mythic struggle between good and evil, the
> stretching risks of adventure, the power of role play,
> drama and the social skills learnt in the game. The dimin-
> ishment in contemporary Britain of safe space in which to
> play is the biggest single threat to the freedom and
> creativity which are the secret of a full childhood. Why
> not build an adventure playground in the churchyard or
> a children's nature study centre at the diocesan retreat
> house? Perhaps this would be better than keeping the
> children out of the graveyard or off the grass.[434]

- A shelter for the homeless supported by CUF with matched
  funding and leaders drawn from housing, health and homelessness agencies. Established initially in the church rooms
  before independent premises were acquired.
- A forum that brought clergy and laity together to discuss the
  social implications of Christian believing in the context of
  Hull city centre. It was entitled the Rerum Novarum Group,
  based on the centenary of the Papal Encyclical (1891) and
  included university and industrial chaplains, a diocesan
  social responsibility officer, and the leader of the City
  Council.[435]

These partnerships promoted a more effective community but
also a more effective church, reflecting the slogan 'a more
effective church in a more effective community'.[436]
Specifically, they:

- encouraged a new confidence in a local congregation in relation to mission and service, through visible evidence of growth in the membership and direct contact with the wider locality
- facilitated deeper trust and co-operation between the church and local agencies in the pursuit of a common agenda premised on local needs and issues
- achieved measurable outcomes in relation to the provision of new amenities and facilities for a range of clients and users that had not previously been available
- contributed to the numerical growth of the congregation: parents of children joined the church; members of the Sunday Club became occasional worshippers; key workers from local agencies,[437] initially encouraged by the readiness of the church to share in projects then sought a deeper involvement that led to full membership; attendance at Sunday morning worship grew slowly to more than 30 and a nucleus of worshippers shared in the Eucharist each Tuesday evening.

Partnerships therefore provided one strategic approach that sought to establish 'a broad and living way . . . into the hearts of the people'.[438] It was complemented by a disciplined spirituality, a commitment to catholicity of spirit in relation to worship, and fellowship based on mutual respect and service, and a preparedness to introduce outsiders into the church's life through visiting, a weekly newsletter and special services. It enabled a congregation to change lives for the better and emphasized the foundational role of a local church as both embodiment and promoter of civil society.[439] It facilitated a more extensive use of the church building without any harmful erosion of its ethos as a place of worship that sought to embrace the excluded. And it made possible a better understanding of the realities of urban life as in themselves constituting a necessary part of the theological task.

In a modest way this UPA church demonstrated the hallmarks of the strategic approach to mission adumbrated in

Changing Church and Society in Chapter 4. It reflected a distinctiveness nurtured in a tradition of Anglo-Catholic worship yet was porous enough at its boundaries to avoid the danger of exclusivity.[440] Its building, rooms and human resources were engaged to develop a more effective presence in the locality and, without jettisoning valued traditions, it looked forward with expectation to God's future.

The one caveat I am inclined to register in relation to this approach concerns the potential danger of a local church being taken over by more powerful partners. As Local Strategic Partnerships[441] impact on marginalized communities, there is a need to ensure that what are perceived by others as practical solutions for specific problems are also to some degree compatible with the distinctive values, concerns and needs of the local church.[442] Atherton comments that this will require:

> a clarity of understanding and the proclamation of Christian identity in such partnership, recognizing, for example, that the government's promotion of faith community involvement in partnership is now valued not simply because of its practical contributions but also because of what the faith dimension itself can and should bring to such work.[443]

Taking some words from Isaiah, the requirement now is that partners should 'come and reason together' (1.18) for the sake of economic and social regeneration. Such an exercise is in itself a demonstration of public theology at work, acknowledging the complexity of things at the local level and working with what is available to enhance the civic good in such a way that the needs of the most vulnerable are recognized and addressed. Partnership is about making connections and the realization that: 'There is one world and it is not endless and we have to work out among ourselves how we are to live in it together or we shall die in it separately.'[444]

Partnership is about risk and the readiness to learn how God, through others, invites us to celebrate our common humanity.

Deep, Difficult, Holy Work

In this last section we end where we began our exploration of
urban mission – in the nineteenth century amid Christ's poor.
The title comes from the writings of Josephine Butler, a devout
Christian and woman of prayer basing her spirituality on that
of Catherine of Siena, whose biography she wrote. Josephine
was also an activist and reformer, concerned for the plight of
prostitutes, heavily involved in the work of women's education in Liverpool and with a keen eye for legislation that was
socially repressive or unjust. She died in 1906. Throughout
her long and eventful life she never lost sight of the importance
of the individual and the necessity on the part of the Church to
engage in 'deep, difficult, holy work' for the sake of the poor.

More than a century on, this still strikes me with the force
of an imperative. So much has changed: the post-millennium
city assumes ever more perplexing configurations and I have
argued that theological acuity, prayer, worship, the promotion
of civil society and partnerships represent the way forward for
urban mission. Yet we must also be committed to the work
of love, the deep, difficult holy love of Christ which visibly
expended itself for the sake of others (Phil. 2.1–11). One thing
we know is that whatever the shape or direction of the emerging urban order, not everyone will share in its wealth
or conviviality. During a conversation at Union Theological
Seminary, a final-year student commented to me: 'By all
means deconstruct the city. But always remember that beyond
image and text there are marginalized people who must
remain central to our concern.'[445]

Her words were a moving reminder to me that the hungry
and poor should not be forgotten (Ps. 9.18), that the individual
should never be lost as we work alongside others to renew the
city. They were also a challenge to carry on unselfishly in the
recognition that we are bound together in a common life:

> This above all is remarkable
> How we put ourselves in one another's care
> How in spite of everything, we trust each other.[446]

Intimations of civil society again despite all the pressures towards the impersonal and social fragmentation. And something else – the realization that the Christian way of living in this world did not begin with an idea, a philosophy or a set of moral propositions.[447] It began in particular events – birth, teaching, healing, passion, death and resurrection – life-changing actions so vast and deep in their import that others could do no other but speak of them in awe and amazement:

> That which was from the beginning, which we have heard, which we have seen with our eyes, which we have looked at and our hands have touched – this we proclaim concerning the Word of life. The life appeared; we have seen it and testify to it, and we proclaim to you the eternal life, which was with the Father and has appeared to us. We proclaim to you what we have seen and heard, so that you also may have fellowship with us. And our fellowship is with the Father and with his Son, Jesus Christ. We write this to make our joy complete. (1 John 1.1–4)

The One of whom the New Testament speaks in such eloquent terms always seems to find the individual among the crowds in the city: desperate Zacchaeus seeking affirmation; blind Bartimaeus longing for his sight; the woman caught in the act of adultery; the boy with loaves and fishes whose slight provisions feed a multitude. For us to do the will of Christ now in the urban will require action that is concrete, small-scale and intensely personal, representing a commitment to the vivifying memory of One who made time to admire the lilies of the field and tells us that not even a sparrow falls to the ground without his Father's knowledge.

If partnerships necessarily involve us in matters of contextual analysis and social policy that shape the lives of entire communities, the work of practical compassion will address itself to particularity – to the individual, to precarious hopes and the possibilities of human worth and dignity.[448] Its primary concern will be to serve and affirm people where they are, particularly those born into disadvantage and who struggle to survive. In so doing we seek to emulate the example of One who came 'not to be served but to serve and to give his life as a ransom for many' (Matt. 20.28). What this amounts to in practical and personal terms was given memorable expression in a sermon preached by Eric Treacy, former Bishop of Wakefield, at the institution of a new parish priest. Describing some of the private griefs common to any local community and drawing on his own experience of urban ministry, he elaborated the meaning of service to others in the name of Christ:

> It means sharing the suffering of a father and mother with one very precious daughter aged 12 who is dying of cancer. It means dealing with the schizophrenic woman tortured with a persecution mania and convinced her husband is trying to poison her. It means listening to a woman who has twice tried to commit suicide because she cannot face the loneliness of widowhood and may try to do it again. It means rampaging round the Town Hall trying to get an eviction order cancelled for an unemployed miner because he hasn't paid his rent. It means sharing the grief of the bereaved, the suffering of the hospital ward, the misery and defeat of the prison cell. It means being so identified with Christ's love for your people that everything that happens to them in some measure happens to you. It means having strength and confidence sufficient to give others so they can face life and death without fear.[449]

The doing of love's work constitutes an unfinished agenda and always calls us back to what matters in the real world. Whether it is a soup run for the homeless, a drop-in centre for the lonely, lifts for the housebound or assisting asylum seekers with bewildering forms,[450] in each case there is the tacit acknowledgement that where there is need there is also for the local church an obligation.

I am aware of the limitations and dangers of this approach. It can unwittingly patronize the recipients and leave untouched the fundamentally unjust systems that perpetuate poverty. Laurie Green has reminded us that although compassion, care and loving service are wonderful qualities, 'they are attributes which we thankfully share with all humanity'.[451] For him, the distinctive contribution of Christian faith – the necessary addition to pastoral care – is to find ways of helping people to ask important questions of their society so that new and better patterns of community and civil society can emerge.[452] In a similar vein, David Nicholls has chided those who are reluctant to challenge existing structures, who suppose that caring is enough and that the common good can be realized if people would only behave a bit more reasonably. For them the kingdom will come 'slowly, silently and peacefully and . . . the mighty will be lowered so gently from their seats as not to feel the bump when they reach the ground'.[453]

The remark is gently disarming and my hope is that I have provided sufficient evidence in the previous chapters of my own conviction that the duty to care for others must always be accompanied by critical reflection on the wider issues that are shaping the destiny of our planet and our cities. Yet I am also aware that my experience in Hull, replicated in other UPAs, of dealing with an increasing number of those who are trying to survive, also means that sometimes there is less time to consider what is causing such injustices. Margaret Walsh comments pithily: 'It is difficult "to act justly, love tenderly and walk humbly with your God" all at the same time'.[454] I take this to mean that when hard choices frequently have to be made we must honour the religious conviction that the person in need is the neighbour given us to love as ourselves as a matter of the highest priority – more important even than the high work of prayer. I gain help and comfort here from St Vincent de Paul who in his own lifetime worked for the relief of galley slaves, victims of war and convicts and helped to establish religious communities devoted to the poor and sick:

The service of the poor is to be preferred to all else, and to be performed without delay. If at a time set aside for prayer, medicine or help has to be brought to some poor person, go and do what has to be done with an easy mind, offering it up to God as a prayer. Do not be put out by uneasiness or a sense of sin because of prayers interrupted by the service of the poor: for God is not neglected if prayers are put aside, if the work of God is interrupted, in order that another such work may be completed.

Therefore, when you leave prayer to help some poor remember this – that the work has been done for God. Charity takes precedence over all rules, everything ought to tend to it since it is itself a great lady: what it orders should be carried out. Let us show our service to the poor, then, with renewed ardour in our hearts, seeking out in particular any destitute people, since they are given to us as lords and patrons.[455]

The Christian communities that I have described in these pages – in Merseyside, Wolverhampton and Hull, and others like them – testify to the potential in every person and a shared resolve to act in hope. And by helping the damaged and excluded to rediscover their humanity, they also demonstrate that small groups of Christians can make a real difference far exceeding their numerical strength. Such communities know the importance of the margin and the necessity of prayer and worship. They offer a ministry of presence and imagination and embody a distinctive character that speaks of confidence and vulnerability. Forty years ago, Monica Furlong gave a paper to the Wakefield Diocesan Conference. Her words now seem remarkably prescient in relation to what we have to do and *be* in the crucible of the urban:

I want them to be people who are secure enough in the value of what they are doing to have time to read, to sit and think, and who can face the emptiness and possible depression which often attack people when they do not keep the surface of their mind occupied. I want them to be people who have faced this kind of loneliness and discovered how fruitful it is, as I want them to be people who have faced the problems of prayer. I want them to be people who can sit still without feeling guilty and from whom I can learn some kind of tranquillity in a society which has almost lost the art.[456]

Deep, difficult, holy work only becomes possible and, in the long term, sustainable through this kind of formation that touches heart and mind at the deepest level and constitutes a lifetime's work. Furlong was addressing the clergy but her remarks seem to me required reading for anyone contemplating or undertaking a serious engagement with the city in the name of Christ. To say 'I believe' in the face of everything the urban represents in terms of earthly possibilities and tragedies (and not least our own waywardness) is, of necessity, to remember that the Latin *credo* has at its root the word *cor* (heart). To say *credo* therefore means much more than mere utterance or even careful assent to specific formulations of faith: it is to set our heart towards God in the face of One who challenges us to a more genuine understanding of ourselves and a more compassionate engagement with the lost and rejected:

> Can you drink of this cup?
> The cup I drink.
> Cup of sorrow.
> Can you bear betrayal, desertion, despair?
> Can you drink of this cup,
> Cup of sin.
> Can you see your own face,
> Reflected in the wine?
> Can you see your own life,
> Caught in the cup?
> Cup of sacrifice.
> Can you drink of this cup?
> The cup I drink.
> Cup of solace.

Can you share compassion, companionship, hope?
Can you drink of this cup,
Cup of acceptance.
Can you see your own face,
Reflected in the wine?
Can you see your own life,
Caught in the cup?
Cup of rejoicing.[457]

Postscript

These final lines fall on a significant day – the anniversary
of my ordination and, later this evening, a lecture on urban
mission to be given to a gathering of Church of England
Readers. All is prepared and there will be some reference to
the material between these pages. To enliven the proceedings
on a hot summer night the overhead projector will be put to
good use: there are pictures of Babel; powerful images of
Christ crucified and risen; intimations of the New Jerusalem;
words from Jeremiah urging us 'to seek the welfare of the city'
and a dramatic shot of the New York harbour skyline before
11 September 2001, seemingly unassailable with its twin
towers thrusting to the heavens. There is a striking portrait
of John Henry Newman to remind my audience of the
Oxford Movement and the holiness of life it excited among
clergy encountering the worst depredations of industrial life
more than a century ago. And there is a representation of St
Augustine bearing his episcopal staff, clutching a sacred text
and gazing impassively, it seems, towards some distant vista. I
intend to spend a fair amount of time on this particular image.

Augustine impresses me deeply. He was a theologian of formidable intellectual power; a pastor immersed in the lives and
struggles of his clergy and congregations; a black man from
urban North Africa[458] in a time of great social turbulence as
the old civilization of Greece and Rome began to pass away
and the Dark Ages drew on. Across the centuries his voice and
example bring a word of reassurance as we engage with change

and upheaval and our cities are often seen as repositories for all that is awful in the modern world. We need to remember that this great leader of the Church was also considered peripheral in his day – 'a provincial on the margins of classical culture'[459] – one of almost seven hundred bishops in Africa alone.[460] We may think of him in episcopal finery but he would have dressed in the grey clothes of a monk and celebrated the liturgy in those same garments. Faced with the calamity of the sack of Rome by the Goths in 410, he did not despair or shirk the mental task of how some sort of meaning could be derived from apparent desolation.[461] He wrote instead, the *City of God (De Civitate Dei)*. Amid the clamour of his age and a world in apparent ruin he looked, and taught others to look, beyond decline:

> At this time Rome was overwhelmed in disaster after its capture by the Goths under their king Alaric. Those who worship the multitude of false gods, whom we usually call pagans, tried to lay the blame for the disaster on the Christian religion, and began to blaspheme the true God more fiercely and bitterly than before. This fired me with zeal for the house of God and I began to write the *City of God* to confute their blasphemies and falsehood. This took a number of years for other tasks intervened . . . but the great work . . . was at last finished in twenty-two books.[462]

It took him 13 years to write by which time he was 72. Four years later with the Vandal hordes swarming over Africa, he died at the besieged seaport of Hippo. Almost miraculously his library and writings survived intact.

Augustine matters because he was and is an encourager. To demoralized Christians surrounded by paganism and wracked by uncertainty he gave a sense of identity, 'told them where they belonged, to what they must be loyal'.[463] In a time of crisis he told them not to fear but to 'regain your youth in Christ'.[464] He urged them to form 'a partnership with the past' and feel their individual and collective strength when things went awry:

> Each generation thinks its own time, uniquely awful; that morality and religion have never been at so low an ebb . . . and civilized values have never been more threatened. But whether times are good or bad depends on the moral quality of individual and social life and it is up to us.[465]

Augustine calls us to unceasing reflection on how things are in the world. His own thought was dynamic – Karl Jaspers describes him as someone 'who thinks in questions' – and throughout his writings there is evidence of a mind refashioning what it found inadequate and continually pressing on towards the search for truth and clarity. He would have understood very well the task of the *bricoleur* and our contemporary need for careful social analysis in the city. He was also on the side of the poor and, while recognizing the need for the Church to provide its daily soup kitchen, insisted on social justice: 'Take away justice and what are governments but gangsters on a large scale.'[466] He saw that urban life embraces not one but two realities – the earthly city and the city of God – and 'the two are intertwined and intermixed in the world until they be separated by the final judgement'.[467] In the meantime our business is emphatically 'within this common mortal life'[468] working for positive change, avoiding greater evils and being genuinely grateful for the favourable conditions it provides. To the surprise of many perhaps who are acquainted with Augustine only through his more sombre writings on predestination and original sin, he was incarnational in his thinking, committed to the essential goodness of created things and delighting in their beauty. All these were gifts: '*bona . . . dona* is a key phrase throughout the *City of God* . . . who is thought of as a lavisher of gifts'.[469]

We have an embarrassment of riches in these varied teachings and, equally important, the example of a great Christian soul emphasizing the need for gratitude on our part for the unceasing good that still flows beside evil 'as in a vast racing river'.[470] Now as then we find ourselves in the centre of what Francis Fukuyama has described as the Great Disruption. None of us can see too clearly where our present social upheaval will lead or how it will end. We know only, following Augustine, that our confusions and uncertainties about the city exist within a world of grace – God's kingdom. Sustained by 'Christ, the living bread' and the consummation of a hope that is still eagerly awaited[471] we are to work patiently for the refashioning of the Church and the rebuilding of community. In the words of Zechariah – 'Old men and old women shall again sit in the streets of Jerusalem, each with staff in hand for very age. And the streets of the city shall be full of boys and girls playing in its streets' (Zech. 8.4–5). The prophets and Augustine sustained this vision in the darkest of times. In our own unsettled urban dispensation they summon us to do the same:

> Walk about Zion, go round about her,
> number her towers,
> consider well her ramparts,
> go through her citadels;
> that you may tell the next generation
> that this is God,
> our God for ever and ever.
> He will be our guide even unto death. (Ps. 48.12–14)

Notes

Chapter 1

1. A. Nevins (ed.), *Diary of John Quincy Adams 1794–1845*, Charles Scribner's Sons, 1951, p. 177.

2. For an account of the 1851 religious census, see O. Chadwick, *The Victorian Church*, Part 1, A. & C. Black, 1966, pp. 363–9.

3. See A. Wilkinson, *Christian Socialism: Scott Holland to Tony Blair*, SCM Press, 1998, p. 14.

4. C. J. Stranks, *Dean Hook*, Mowbray, 1954, p. 93.

5. E. R. Norman, *Church and Society in England 1770–1970*, Oxford University Press, 1976, p. 132.

6. Comment made to Church Congress held at York 1866 by Robert Bickersteth, formerly incumbent of a large London parish for many years. See *Authorised Report of the Proceedings of the Church Congress held at York*, 1866, York, 1867, p. 61.

7. See for e.g. S. Best, *Parochial Ministrations*, J. Hatchard & Son, 1839, pp. 24–40.

8. Norman, *Church and Society*, p. 128.

9. Source: S. Ayling, *John Wesley*, Collins, 1979, p. 317.

10. Quotation of George Borrow. See Chadwick, *Victorian Church*, Part 1, p. 391.

11. Duly noted in the *Official Report of the 1886 Church Congress*, London, 1886, p. 269.

12. The rallying cry for the Oxford Movement was a sermon on 'National Apostasy' in 1833 by John Keble. The movement owed much to the inspiration of John Henry Newman and the Tractarians who wrote in defence of their High Church doctrines. See Chadwick, *Victorian Church*, Part I, pp. 64–75.

13. Quoted in *The Church Times*, 18 December 1987. One outstanding example was that of Lincoln Stanhope Wright who at the age of 26 arrived in Wapping on Low Sunday 1873 to serve the mission church of St Peter's, London Docks. He spent the remaining 56 years of his life in this slum parish, sleeping on a straw mattress in an uncarpeted room and

never taking a holiday. See A. N. Wilson, *The Victorians*, Hutchinson, 2002, p. 365.

14. The Poor Law Amendment Act of 1834 abolished the 1601 paupers' right to parish support. The workhouses provided the grimmest form of charity even on the holiest of days: 'On Christmas Day, 1840, in the Eton workhouse, Elizabeth Wyse, a married woman, was allowed the rare privilege of being allowed to comfort her two-and-a-half-year-old daughter because she had chilblains. (The separation of parents and children in the workhouses was automatic, and one of the things which even in the better-run establishments caused most bitterness.) Mrs Wyse was allowed to sleep with her child for one night, but the director of the workhouse (like many of them a former sergeant-major) refused permission for a second night. When the ex-sergeant major, Joseph Howe, found Mrs Wyse in the nursery next day, bathing and bandaging her child's feet, he ordered her to leave the room at once. She refused. He dragged her downstairs, locked her in the workhouse cage, and left her in solitary confinement with no coat, no bedding-straw and no chamber-pot, in 20°F of frost, for twenty-four hours. The following morning she was taken to eat breakfast, which was the remains of cold gruel left by her fellow inmates, and sent back to the cage and told to clean the floor – which was inevitably soiled – but with no utensils to do so' (cited by Wilson, *Victorians*, p. 29).

15. Cited in *The Ashton Standard*, 18 December 1858.

16. In relation to modern Christian social ethics and its response to capitalism, Ronald Preston traces its genesis to 1848 and Maurice's 'recovery of a theological critique of the assumptions behind the social order which had died out with the collapse of traditional Anglican and Puritan moral theology at the end of the seventeenth-century'. See his *Church and Society in the Late Twentieth Century*, SCM Press, 1983, p. 15.

17. F. D. Maurice, *On the Reformation of Society and How All Classes May Contribute to it*, Forbes & Knibb, 1851, pp. 32, 36.

18. Chadwick, *Victorian Church*, Part 1, p. 442.

19. F. D. Maurice, *The Kingdom of Christ*, 1838, Everyman edn, n.d., p. 323.

20. Cited by C. Bryant in *Possible Dreams: A Personal History of the British Christian Socialists*, Hodder & Stoughton, 1997, p. 71.

21. S. D. Headlam, *Christian Socialism*, London, 1892, p. 6.

22. Part of Headlam's, 'Priest's Political Programme', *Church Reformer*, 111, No. 10, October 1884.

23. See S. Paget, *Henry Scott Holland*, John Murray, 1921, p. 170.

24. Taken from CSU Journal *Commonwealth*, 16, No. 182, February 1911, p. 35.

25. Cited by Norman, *Church and Society*, p. 183.

26. See Chadwick, *Victorian Church*, Part 1, pp. 349–51, for an account of their preaching style and the response it elicited.

27. K. Inglis, *Churches and the Working Classes in Victorian England*, Routledge and Kegan Paul, 1963, p. 265.

28. C. Gore (ed.), *Lux Mundi: A Series of Studies in the Religion of the Incarnation*, John Murray, 1889.

29. M. Ramsey, *From Gore to Temple: The Development of Anglican Theology between Lux Mundi and the Second World War 1889–1939*, Longman, 1960, pp. vii–viii.

30. See Gore (ed.), *Lux Mundi*, p. 14.

31. O. Chadwick, *The Victorian Church*, Part 2, A. & C. Black, 1970, p. 296.

32. H. P. Hughes, *Social Christianity*, Hodder & Stoughton, p. 14.

33. Hughes, *Social Christianity*, p. 49.

34. Scholars such as Wayne Meeks and Gerd Theissen set the expansion of early Christianity in a specifically urban context. Meeks describes Paul as a city person, a product of urban Judaism well equipped to assist his fledgling communities as they faced the complexities of urban society in the Roman Empire. See W. Meeks, *The First Urban Christians: The Social World of the Apostle Paul*, Yale University Press, 1983, p. 9. See also G. Theissen, *The Social Setting of Pauline Christianity: Essays on Corinth*, T&T Clark; Fortress Press, 1983. In relation to the impact of the urban on these new Christian communities Stephen Barton notes: 'The ethos of the cities also contributed to the identity and self-understanding of these urban Christians. It is impossible to understand the significance of Paul's boast to "have become all things to all (people)" (1 Corinthians 9.22) outside the context of the pluralism of the Hellenistic city. Nor was this pluralism racial only. The controversies in the Corinthian groups over sexual practice, food taboos, idol worship, and hairstyles all bear witness to the "cultural potpourri" which influenced their style of life.' See S. Barton, 'Paul, Religion and Society', in S. Obelkevich, L. Roper and S. Raphael (eds), *Disciplines of Faith: Studies in Religion, Politics and Patriarchy*, Routledge & Kegan Paul, 1987, p. 170.

35. Extract from letter of Davidson to Scott Holland, 1 February 1906. See *Randall Davidson Papers*, 1906, Lambeth Palace Library.

36. R. Davidson, *The Character and Call of the Church of England*, Macmillan, 1912, p. 119.

37. P. Colson, *Life of the Bishop of London (Winnington-Ingram)*, Jarrolds, 1935, p. 106.

38. J. G. Lockhart, *Cosmo Gordon Lang*, Hodder & Stoughton, 1949, p. 239.

39. *Report of the Anglo-Catholic Congress 1923*, London, 1923, p. 185.

40. See Wilkinson, *Christian Socialism*, p. 64.

41. Wilkinson, *Christian Socialism*, p. 64.

42. Norman, *Church and Society*, p. 251.

43. A. Hastings, *A History of English Christianity 1920–1985*, Collins, 1986, p. 172.

44. 'Very little is said about the work of clergy and laity in the poorest parishes'. Quotation from C. F. Garbett, *In The Heart of South London*, Longman, 1931, p. 132.

45. Twelve commissions were appointed in 1921 by the COPEC Executive Committee; each comprised experts and clergy charged with the responsibility of producing reports that, in the words of William Temple, should be more important than the conference itself. The commissions sent out 200,000 questionnaires.

46. This anecdote is attributed to Charles Raven who was present for the proceedings.

47. *The Proceedings of COPEC: Being a Report of the Meetings of the Conference on Christian Politics, Economics and Citizenship held in Birmingham*, 5–12 April, London, 1924, p. 261.

48. Taken from the proceedings of COPEC, p. 273.

49. The quotation is taken from the objects of COPEC printed after 1921 in a rectangular enclosure at the top of Temple's notepaper. For a full account of COPEC's deliberations and the reports under consideration see Norman, *Church and Society*, pp. 290–308.

50. F. A. Iremonger, *Men and Movements in the Church: A Series of Interviews*, Longman, 1928, p. 28.

51. See Bryant, *Possible Dreams*, p. 244.

52. Almost three million people were unemployed in 1931. See B. B. Gilbert, *British Social Policy 1914–39*, Batsford, 1970, pp. 166–74.

53. Hastings, *A History of English Christianity*, p. 258.

54. William Temple, *Christianity and Social Order*, Penguin, 1942. Cited in *A Summary of Unemployment and the Future of Work: An Enquiry for the Churches*, CCBI, 1997, p. 7.

55. M. Ramsey, *Durham Essays and Addresses*, SPCK, 1956, p. 41.

56. Hastings, *A History of English Christianity*, p. 349.

57. R. Preston, 'A Bishop ahead of his Church', in R. J. Elford and I. S. Markham (eds), *The Middle Way: Theology, Politics and Economics in the Late Thought of R. H. Preston*, SCM Press, 2000, p. 25.

58. E. R. Wickham, *Church and People in an Industrial City*, Lutterworth, 1957.

59. D. Sheppard, *Bias to the Poor*, Hodder & Stoughton, 1983.

60. Cited by David Sheppard in 'Our Faith in the City', *The Tablet*, 11 December 1999, pp. 1,676–7.

61. See R. Preston, 'Not out of the Wood Yet', in R. J. Elford and I. S.

Markham (eds), *The Middle Way: Theology, Politics and Economics in the Late Thought of R. H. Preston*, SCM Press, 2000, pp. 88–9.

Chapter 2

62. *Faith in the City: A Call for Action by Church and Nation*, Church House Publishing, 1985.

63. See comments of Peter Bruinvels, MP for Leicester East and General Synod Member, in A. Hastings, *Robert Runcie*, Mowbray, 1991, p. 93.

64. See John Vincent in 'Wanted – an Urban Theology', 1993, p. 1. Cited in P. Sedgwick (ed.), *God in the City: Essays and Reflections from the Archbishop of Canterbury's Urban Theology Group*, Mowbray, 1995, p. 16.

65. To date grants of more than £47 million have been awarded covering 3,600 projects meeting a wide spectrum of social need. Source: Church Urban Fund, January 2003.

66. B. Abel-Smith and P. Townsend, *The Poor and the Poorest*, Occasional Papers in Social Administration, No. 17, G. Bell & Sons Ltd, 1965.

67. S. Becker and S. MacPherson (eds), *Public Issues Private Pain: Poverty, Social Work and Social Policy*, Social Services Insight Books Care Matters Ltd, 1988, p. 3.

68. CPAG also became a very effective political pressure group under the leadership of Frank Field.

69. See P. Townsend (ed.), *The Concept of Poverty*, Heinemann, 1970, p. ix.

70. P. Townsend, *Poverty in the United Kingdom: A Survey of Household Resources and Standards of Living*, Allen Lane Penguin Books, 1979, p. 31.

71. There have been sporadic attempts since 1979 to deny the validity of the concept of relative poverty, usually by right-wing politicians or economists. To give two examples: in 1979 Keith Joseph commented: 'An absolute standard means one defined by reference to the actual needs of the poor and not by reference to the expenditure of those who are not poor. A family is poor if it cannot afford to eat.' See K. Joseph and J. Sumption, *Equality*, John Murray, 1979, p. 27. Ten years later, the then Secretary of State for Social Security, John Moore, was still describing relative concepts of poverty as 'bizarre'. See J. Moore, 'The End of the Line for Poverty', speech to the Greater London Conservative Party Conference, 11 May 1989, cited by H. Russell, in *Poverty Close to Home: A Christian Understanding*, Mowbray, 1995, p. 44.

72. For examples see *Public Issues Private Pain*, pp. 5–13.

73. *Faith in the City*, p. 330. 14.9.

74. P. Harrison, *Inside the Inner City: Life under the Cutting Edge*, Penguin, 1983.

75. *The Brixton Disorders 10th–12th April 1981*, HMSO, 1981, Cmnd 8427, para. 8.48.

76. A Home Office Study published in 1982 found no evidence to refute this assertion. See Roger Torling, *Unemployment and Crime*, Home Office Research and Planning Unit, 1982.

77. The then Secretary of State for Health, Patrick Jenkin, conceded in a foreword to the report (DHSS 1980) that the recommendations could not be accepted because they were too expensive to implement. A shorter version of the report was published later by the Health Education Council. A press conference to mark its publication was cancelled by its Director General: 'There were strong denials that ministers had in any way tried to influence the abandonment of the press-conference, but it seemed to me that the very strength of the denials implied they were untrue.' Part of an interview given by Sir Douglas Black in *The Oldie Magazine*, 106, January 1998, pp. 21–2. For commentary on the original report, see P. Townsend, N. Davidson and M. Whitehead (eds), *Inequalities in Health: The Black Report: The Health Divide*, Penguin, 1990.

78. E. Hobsbawm, *Age of Extremes: The Short Twentieth Century 1914–1991*, Michael Joseph, 1994, p. 408.

79. The views of the New Right were promulgated in the publications of the Centre for Policy Studies founded by Mrs Thatcher in 1974.

80. Comment made in interview in *Woman's Own* magazine, October 1987.

81. J. Raban, *God, Man and Mrs Thatcher*, Chatto & Windus, 1989, pp. 54–6.

82. Adrian Hastings views *Faith in the City* as the most important venture of Runcie's tenure as Archbishop of Canterbury: 'the enterprise in which he affected the most people, was most attacked and most justified, the venture for which he is in the long run likely to be most remembered' (*Robert Runcie*, Mowbray, 1991, p. 91).

83. Hastings, *Robert Runcie*, p. 91.

84. Letter published in *The Times*, 27 May 1981.

85. The group included David Sheppard of Liverpool and Stanley Booth-Clibborn of Manchester. See Hastings, *Robert Runcie*, p. 92.

86. Sir Richard O'Brien, a retired senior civil servant, chaired the inquiry. Secretarial support was seconded from the Department of the Environment to indicate the 'civil' dimensions of the work to be undertaken. Other members were drawn from senior church positions, UPAs, academia, industry and the voluntary and public sector. Together they brought valuable experience and a high degree of professional

competence to their common task. Some had written books on a range of related subjects; others were involved with organizations working in the cities or knew what it was like from first-hand experience to live in a UPA. Over a longer period members met 17 times and received 283 written submissions from a wide range of agencies and individuals. Crucially, they also spent time visiting many of the areas under consideration.

87. Hastings, *Robert Runcie*, p. 92.

88. *Faith in the City*, p. xv.

89. This summary is based on the assessment of the report provided by H. Russell in *Keeping Faith with the Cities: A Publication to Mark the Tenth Anniversary of Faith in the City*, Christian Socialist Movement, 1995, p. 3.

90. *Faith in the City*, p. 74.

91. *Faith in the City*, pp. 97–8, 5.62.

92. See *Living Faith in the City*, General Synod Publications, 1990, p. 12.

93. *Faith in the City*, p. 56. 3.17.

94. *Faith in the City*, p. 57. 3.18.

95. *Faith in the City*, p. 59. 3.22.

96. *Faith in the City*, p. 70.

97. *Faith in the City*, p. 360.

98. *Faith in the City* sold in excess of 50,000 copies and was even translated into some European languages.

99. Speech in the House of Lords 12 February 1987. Cited by Hastings, *Robert Runcie*, p. 95.

100. See K. Leech, *Struggle in Babylon: Racism in the Cities and Churches of Britain*, Sheldon Press, 1988, pp. 135–6.

101. See G. Moody, 'Life in the City', in P. Sedgwick (ed.), *God in the City*, Mowbray, 1995, pp. 9–15, p. 12.

102. See *Powerful Whispers*, Bradford Faith in the City Forum, 1995.

103. *Seeds of Hope in the Parish*, Church House Publishing, 1996.

104. See H. Russell (ed.), *The Servant Church in Granby*, Centre for Urban Studies, University of Liverpool, 1989, p. 21.

105. The commission saw its work proceeding from 'a long tradition of Christian social concerns . . . with notable examples in the nineteenth century of church leaders . . . being so shocked by the social conditions of the time that they worked energetically for change', *Faith in the City*, pp. 56–7.

106. *Faith in the City*, p. 49, 3.7.

107. Russell, *Keeping Faith with the Cities*, p. 118.

108. Comments made during my interview with the ICRC Secretary, 30 May 1996. The Government met all the support costs of the council estimated at £200,000 p.a. The secretary's salary was met by

contributions from the Church of England, Methodist, Roman Catholic and black-led churches.

109. Cited by B. Rippin, Chairman of Sheffield District of the Methodist Church and Free Church representative on the ICRC. See his 'Inner Cities Religious Council', *Poverty Network*, 20, September 1993, pp. 23–4.

110. In her memoir Mary Warnock describes Thatcherism as 'not really a philosophy but an outflowing of prejudice . . . to gratify a Conservative Party that had need of a specific theory with which to counter socialism'. M. Warnock, *A Memoir: People and Places*, Duckworth, 2000. Quotation taken from review in *The Tablet*, 6 January 2001, p. 17.

111. See for e.g. H. Willmer, 'Images of the City and the Shaping of Humanity', in A. Harvey (ed.), *Theology in the City*, SPCK, 1989, pp. 32–46.

112. Letter to *The Church Times*, 14 January 2000.

113. *The Cities: A Methodist Report*, NCH Action for Children, 1997, p. 40.

114. Willmer, 'Images of the City', p. 33.

115. 'Worship is a vital source of resistance and of energy in facing the social evils of violent conflict and rejection which are the daily realities of life at the local parish level.' M. Northcott, 'Worship in the City', in M. Northcott (ed.), *Urban Theology: A Reader*, Cassell, 1998, pp. 221–54, p. 224.

116. *Faith in the City*, pp. 135–8.

117. *Living Faith in the City*, p. 24.

118. See D. Ford, 'Transformation', in P. Sedgwick (ed.), *God in the City*, Mowbray, 1995, pp. 199–209, p. 201. David Ford has provided theological reflections on Ephesians (see above) and Corinthians concerning their relevance to urban mission. See his 'Faith in the Cities: Corinth and the Modern City', in C. Gunton and D. Hardy (eds), *On Being the Church: Essays on the Christian Community*, T&T Clark, 1989, pp. 225–6. For other current examples see N. T. Wright's 'The Letter to the Galatians: Exegesis and Theology', in J. B. Green and M. Turner (eds), *Between Two Horizons: Spanning New Testament Studies and Systematic Theology*, W. B. Eerdmans, 2000, pp. 205–36, pp. 221–30; L. Green 'Why Do Theological Reflection?', in M. Northcott (ed.), *Urban Theology: A Reader*, Cassell, 1998, pp. 11–18, pp. 15–17; A. Davey, *Urban Christianity and Global Order: Theological Resources for an Urban Future*, SPCK, 2001, pp. 58–86.

119. The Chief Rabbi, Dr Jonathan Sacks, describes history as 'the moral tutor of humanity'. Comment made during Radio 4 interview, 16 April 2000. The philosopher Anthony O'Hear has also warned of the

danger of absolutizing the present by an uncritical acceptance of the pervasive notion 'that we can become enlightened if only we purge ourselves of the prejudices of the past'. See his *After Progress: Finding the Old Way Forward*, Bloomsbury, 1999, p. 9.

Chapter 3

120. More than 80 per cent of the population now live in places that are irreversibly urban in character with a minimum population of approximately 1,000 persons. See L. Greenhalgh and K. Worpole, 'The Convivial City', in G. Mulgan (ed.), *Life after Politics: New Thinking for the Twenty-first Century*, Fontana Press, 1997, pp. 167–76, p. 167.

121. See A. Davey, 'London as Theological Problem', *Theology*, CI, No. 801, May/June 1998, pp. 188–96, p. 188.

122. See G. Ward, *Cities of God*, Routledge, 2000, pp. 38–40.

123. See Ward, *Cities*, pp. 212–15, and M. Serres, *Angels: A Modern Myth*, Flammarion, 1993.

124. Ward, *Cities*, p. 28.

125. Ward, *Cities*, p. 28.

126. Josh. 3.4.

127. E. Hobsbawm, *Age of Extremes: The Short Twentieth Century 1914–1991*, Michael Joseph, 1994, p. 4.

128. Christians are called by Christ to read the signs of the times. He rebukes the Pharisees and Sadducees who desired that he would show them a sign from heaven, saying, 'O ye hypocrites, ye can discern the face of the sky; but can ye not discern the signs of the times?' (Matt. 16.3).

129. Ward, *Cities*, pp. 2–3.

130. See Ward, *Cities*, p. 242.

131. For example: eight Regional Development Agencies to administer the SRB and European Regeneration money; Social Exclusion Unit ensuring that all policies that may have a bearing on social exclusion, including urban renewal, are part of an integrated strategy incorporating health, education and crime policy; New Deal for Communities to bring together investment in buildings and people; the launching of pilot projects in 17 cities designated as Pathfinder Areas; Local Government Association's New Commitment to Regeneration – a five-year programme covering 22 authorities which will devise bottom-up strategies; Health Action Zones, Education Action Zones and Employment Zones, all of which are to be linked to regeneration programmes.

132. *Bringing Britain Together: A National Strategy for Neighbourhood Renewal*, SEU, TSO, 1998. The report responded to the Prime Minister's remit to examine 'how to develop integrated and sustainable approaches to the problems of the worst housing estates, including crime, drugs, unemployment, community breakdown and bad schools

etc.'. See *National Strategy for Neighbourhood Renewal*, p. 15, 1.

133. *National Strategy for Neighbourhood Renewal: A Framework for Consultation*, SEU, April 2000.

134. *National Strategy*, pp. 8–9.

135. *Our Towns and Cities: The Future. Delivering on Urban Renaissance*, DETR, The Stationery Office, November 2000. Three other documents were also published with the White Paper: B. Robson, M. Parkinson, M. Boddy and D. MacLennan, *The State of English Cities*, Department of the Environment, Transport and the Regions, Economic and Social Research Council Cities Programme; J. Todorovic and S. Wellington, *Living in Urban England: Attitudes and Aspirations*, Department of the Environment, Transport and the Regions; and *The Government's Response to the Eleventh Report of the Select Committee on Environment, Transport and Regional Affairs: Proposed Urban White Paper*.

136. R. Rogers and A. Power, *Cities for a Small Country*, Faber & Faber, 2000, cited in *Our Towns and Cities*, p. 137.

137. *Our Towns and Cities*, p. 137.

138. Cited in 'Time for an Urban Renaissance', *The New Statesman*, Special Supplement, 26 April 1999, p. 3.

139. 'An important part of such coherence must derive from *less ambiguity in the targeting of resources*. There is a strong argument for the development of an urban budget which might be administered at regional level so as to reflect the varying constraints and opportunities across different regions and to improve co-ordination across programmes and departments.' Extract from B. Robson, *Assessing the Impact of Urban Policy*, HMSO, 1994, Executive Summary, p. xv.

140. See *Socio-demographic Change and the Inner City*, DOE, 1995, p. 99.

141. Writing in *The Times*, 24 April 2001, William Rees-Mogg comments that for people in the wider country beyond the cities 'the urban values . . . of new Labour seem restless, modernist, superficial, hedonistic and agnostic. The countryside perceives its own culture as growing the roots of the English community while it recognises the flowering of the cities. Roots last for centuries. Flowers can fade in a day.' The Urban White Paper, by contrast, acknowledges that although 'real differences exist between rural and urban communities . . . what binds them together is greater than the differences. Each has much to offer the other'. See *Our Towns and Cities*, p. 14.1.6.

142. See for example: (1) Peter Willmott and Robert Hutchinson (eds), *Urban Trends 1: A Report on Britain's Deprived Urban Areas*, Policy Studies Institute, 1992, pp. 81–2; and (2) Peter Willmott (ed.), *Urban Trends 2: A Decade in Britain's Deprived Urban Areas*, Policy

Notes 59

Studies Institute, 1994, pp. 104–6. The final paragraph of the Conclusion reads: 'Thus in our view the government needs to do two things. It should maintain rather than reduce its support for deprived areas. And it should ensure that an adequate share of resources is deployed to build up capacity, both economic and social in the places where the problems are most acute – the deprived areas of Britain's largest cities.'

143. The survey culminated in the publication of *Unemployment and the Future of Work: An Enquiry for the Churches*, CCBI, 1997.

144. From Introduction to *Unemployment and the Future of Work*, p. 1.

145. See M. Benzeval, K. Judge and M. Whitehead (eds), *Tackling Inequalities in Health: An Agenda for Action*, The King's Fund, 1995.

146. The Task Force was set up in May 1998 and headed by Lord Rogers of Riverside. It took evidence from 300 different bodies and individuals.

147. Extract of memorandum taken from *The Church Times*, 25 February 2000.

148. See 'Time for an Urban Renaissance', p. 4.

149. See their 'New role for the Church in Urban Policy?', *Crucible*, 1994, pp. 142–50.

150. Foreword of *Our Towns and Cities*, p. 5.

151. See Greenhalgh and Worpole, 'Convivial City', p. 172.

152. Interview with the author, 5 June 1996.

153. D. Massey, J. Allen and S. Pile, *City Worlds*, Routledge, 1999, p. vii.

154. *Our Towns and Cities*, p. 13. 1.3.

155. See J. Lovering, 'Global Restructuring and Local Impact', in M. Pacione (ed.), *Britain's Cities: Geographies of Division in Urban Britain*, Routledge, 1997, pp. 15–28.

156. A. Davey, *Urban Christianity and Global Order: Theological Resources for an Urban Future*, SPCK, 2001, p. 3.

157. Cited in W. Keegan, 'Global Winners, Global Losers', *The Tablet*, 24 February 2001, pp. 260–1.

158. Cited in J. Sacks, *The Dignity of Difference: How to Avoid the Clash of Civilizations*, Continuum, 2002, pp. 27–8.

159. In 1998 IBM had a total revenue of 78.5 billion dollars – greater than the GDP of the Czech Republic, New Zealand or Egypt. Source: G. Thompson, 'Economic Globalization?', in D. Held (ed.), *A Globalizing World? Culture, Economics, Politics*, Routledge, 2000, p. 105.

160. See J. R. Short, *The Urban Order*, Blackwell, 1996, p. 83.

161. By the end of the year 2000, 10 per cent of the European Union's Gross Domestic Product will have been generated by services. Source: J. O'Loughlin, 'Between Sheffield and Stuttgart: Amsterdam in an

Integrated Europe and a Competitive World Economy', in L. Deben, W. Heinemeijer and D. van der Vaart (eds), *Understanding Amsterdam: Essays on Economic Vitality, City Life and Urban Form*, Het Spinhuis, 1993.

162. Ward, *Cities*, p. 55.

163. D. Massey, *Space, Place and Gender*, Polity Press; University of Minnesota Press, 1994, p. 149.

164. The Nobel prize-winning economist, Joseph Stiglitz, former chief economist of the World Bank, has criticized the way in which major financial institutions impose unrealistic strategies on failing economies. See his 'Globalism's Discontents', *The American Prospect*, 1–14 January 2002, p. 13.1.

165. See Davey, *Urban Christianity*, p. 117.

166. See J. Friedmann, 'The World City Hypothesis', in P. Knox and P. Taylor (eds), *World Cities in a World-system*, Cambridge University Press, 1995, pp. 317–31.

167. G. Monbiot, *Captive State: The Corporate Takeover of Britain*, Macmillan, 2000, p. 1. The theme of corporate power and exploitation is also addressed by N. Klein, *No Logo*, Flamingo, 2001.

168. See P. Foot, *London Review of Books*, 23, No. 4, 22 February 2001, p. 28.

169. See, for example, C. Hamnett, 'Social Polarisation in Global Cities', *Urban Studies*, 31, No. 3, 1998, pp. 401–24.

170. Quotation from Lord Rogers, Chairman, Urban Task Force, cited in *The Independent*, 10 March 2000.

171. Examples are provided in Short, *Urban Order*, pp. 385–9.

172. Cited by J. W. White, 'The Global City Hypothesis', *Urban Affairs Review*, 33, No. 4, March 1998, pp. 451–77, p. 464.

173. Source: *The Times Business News*, 13 October 1998.

174. J. Atherton, *Public Theology for Changing Times*, SPCK, 2000, p. 99. Commenting on these changes in relation to the population explosion worldwide, Drimmelen notes that 'more than a billion jobs will have to be created over the next ten years to provide an income for all the new job entrants'. See R. Van Drimmelen, *Faith in a Global Economy: A Primer for Christians*, WCC Publications, 1998, pp. 27, 80.

175. See Ward, *Cities*, pp. 239–40, for an account of Manchester's growing reputation as a global city.

176. 'Salford Council seems to be a very good example of a local authority which is putting into practice, the current European prescription for city success' (Ward, *The Cities: A Methodist Report*, NCH Action for children, 1997 p. 101).

177. Source: *The Cities*, pp. 71, 73.

178. Source: *The Cities*, p. 80.

179. The City Pride prospectus emerged from the launch of the Single Regeneration Budget (SRB) with three cities including (Manchester/ Salford) being invited to set out a regeneration strategy and a ten-year vision of the local urban area.

180. See *The Lowry Centre: A Project for the Millennium*, Salford City Council, 1996.

181. J. H. Newman, *Sermons, chiefly on the theory of Religious Belief preached before the University of Oxford*, 2nd edn, Rivington, 1884, p. 208.

182. See T. Hillman, 'Core Cities Push for City Regions', *Clearway Urban: Urban Forum News*, 14, October 1999.

183. Ward, *Cities*, p. 56.

184. 'The city is a container of messages, as well as the messages of themselves, passed through society. The writing of the city also involves the reading of the city. There is no one to one correspondence between the production of its message and its consumption. There are alternative, different and contestatory readings of the city'. (Short, *Urban Order*, p. 395).

185. 'New Strategy for the 21st Century', published on the Internet by the Manchester City Council at <www.manchester.gov.uk/ssd>

186. Ward, *Cities*, pp. 238–9.

187. See S. Sassen, *The Global City: London, New York and Tokyo*, Princeton University Press, 1991, p. 317.

188. Ward, *Cities*, p. 241.

189. Cited by P. Hetherington, 'Dirty Old Towns', *The Guardian*, 12 March 2001.

190. Sacks, *Dignity of Difference*, p. 31.

191. P. Jukes, *A Shout in the Street: An Excursion into the Modern City*, Faber & Faber, 1990, provides a fascinating study in the vitality of thoroughfares and neighbourhoods.

192. The distinction between public and private space raises important issues concerning the *use and control* of the urban landscape. See, for example, L. Bondi, 'Gender, Class and Urban Space: Public and Private Space in Contemporary Urban Landscapes', *Urban Geography*, 19, No. 2, February/March 1998, pp. 160–85.

193. See 'Better Public Spaces', *The New Statesman*, 24 March 2003, pp. vii–viii.

194. *Staying in the City: A Report of the Bishops' Advisory Group on Urban Priority Areas*, Church House Publishing, 1995.

195. The meetings were organized in conjunction with Professor Hilary Russell of the Merseyside Churches' Urban Institute.

196. Meeting, 12 March 1996, Liverpool.

197. Meeting, 12 March 1996.

198. Atherton, *Public Theology*, p. 93.

199. 'We waste a lot of effort duplicating things with different government departments demanding a different set of rules and objectives and simply not talking to each other.' Comment of city council executive cited in P. Hetherington, 'Re-inventing the City', *The Guardian*, 24 November 1999.

200. See Charles Landry, *The Creative City: A Toolkit for Urban Innovators*, Earthscan, 2000. Quotation cited by J. Merrick, 'Urban Renewal's Great Leap Forward', *The Independent*, 22 May 2000.

201. L. Sandercock, *Towards Cosmopolis – Planning for Multicultural Cities*, John Wiley & Sons, 1998, p. 219.

202. 'If we do have to retire from areas of deprivation where the Church so often in the past has been renewed in its spiritual life, that to me is a resignation issue.' Quotation from the Bishop of London, Richard Chartres, cited in 'Eye Witness', *The Independent on Sunday*, 26 August 2001.

203. Tom Sine comments: 'Whilst my postmodern UK Christian friends are very skilled at deconstructing the intellectual assumptions underlying modernity they remain oblivious, like the rest of us, to the myriad ways in which the aspirations and values that accompany modernity and the global economy increasingly define what constitutes the good life and better future.' See his 'Living Justly in a Global Future', *Just Right: The Jubilee Action Magazine*, Issue 8, 2003, pp. 26–7.

204. The various meanings and consequences of globalization continue to generate a wide debate: 'As many scholars have maintained, globalization entails the increasing expression of Western, predominantly American commercial values across various former cultural divisions. At the same time, economic and technological advances – if harnessed properly – can open up opportunities for even marginalized people to become global participants. The perils and promise of globalization make inequality a crucial consideration.' See D. A. Hicks, *Inequality and Christian Ethics*, Cambridge University Press, 2000, p. 45. A critique of globalization in relation to its tendency to increase global inequality is offered by R. Wade, 'Global Inequality, Winners and Losers', *The Economist*, 28 April–4 May 2001, pp. 93–9.

For an account of how global markets can be shown to improve the lives of the world's poorest people, see 'Growth Is Good for the Poor', *The Economist*, 27 May 2000. Paper can be downloaded from <www.worldback.org/research/growth/absddolakray/htm>.

205. See for e.g. Sacks, *Dignity of Difference*, pp. 24–35.

206. 'Who owns the space around us, who controls it, who makes it work for us? In any street there are probably 30 different organizations that have a right to interfere – utilities will dig it up, the telecom firms

will plaster adverts on their phone boxes and the local authority will be reliant on a myriad of largely uninterested contractors. And the upshot is too often a mess.' See 'Better Public Spaces', p. v.

Chapter 4

207. *Financial Times*, 6 November 2001.

208. See e.g. *A New Commitment to Neighbourhood Renewal: National Strategy Action Plan*, Social Exclusion Unit, January 2001.

209. R. Gill, *Churchgoing and Christian Ethics*, Cambridge University Press, 1999, p. 93. In relation to statistical decline, G. Davie notes that 'whatever indicator is selected – electoral roll figures, communicant numbers, baptisms, the proportion of marriages taking place in church or confirmations – a similar picture emerges'. See her *Religion in Britain Since 1945*, Blackwell, 1994, p. 52. Confirmation of this trend into the new millennium is provided by P. Brierley in the *UK Christian Handbook 2000–2001*, HarperCollins, 2000.

210. *Faith in the City*, p. 193, 8.104.

211. 'About half of the paid jobs in the world are held by people who work in one-to-five person enterprises, and in some places the percentage is even higher.' Cited by J. Atherton, *Public Theology for Changing Times*, SPCK, 2000, pp. 101–2. A recent survey in the Sefton Borough of Merseyside showed that 671 people were employed by faith communities that collectively had a total recorded income of £9,711,000. See *Living Faiths in Sefton Report*, Diocese of Liverpool and Sefton Council for Voluntary Services, 2002, p. 24.

212. See M. Weber, *The Protestant Ethic and the Spirit of Capitalism*, Unwin, 1985.

213. National trends are reflected in the statistics below relating to the diocese of Manchester:

Year	1960	2000
Baptisms	19,423	4,210
Confirmations	10,571	1,345 (1999)
Easter Day Communicants	92,450	29,800

See J. Atherton, *Marginalization*, SCM Press, 2003, p. 34.

214. See *Changing Church and Changing Society: Developing a Strategy for Mission in the Urban Priority Areas of the Diocese of Manchester*, Board for Church and Society, 1998, p. 12.3. 4.4.

215. Extract from P. Winn and P. Skirrow, 'Regeneration Strategies – a Theological Critique', paper submitted to Liverpool Diocese, 17 March 1998, p. 6.

216. Opening address at church leaders' meeting in Liverpool, 8 April 2000.

217. See Polly Toynbee, article in *The Guardian*, 12 April 2000, in relation to the launch of the *National Strategy for Neighbourhood Renewal*, covering the worst 3,000 urban districts.

218. Part of keynote address given by John Flamson, European Director for Merseyside for the Government Office, at Faith Communities – Key Partners in Regeneration Conference, Merseyside, 27 March 2003.

219. Winn and Skirrow, 'Regeneration Strategies', pp. 3–4.

220. Extract from P. Winn, 'Why the Church Needs Its UPA Parishes', *The Edge*, Diocese of Liverpool Newsletter, 10, April 2000.

221. See T. Gorringe, *Capital and the Kingdom: Theological Ethics and Economic Order*, Orbis/SPCK, 1994, p. 23.

222. The doctrine of God as creator implies the goodness of creation. The first biblical account of creation records 'And God saw that it was good' (Gen. 1.10, 18, 21, 25, 31). Humanity is also made in God's image (Gen. 1.27) – an idea often expressed with reference to the Latin slogan *imago Dei*. J. O'Donnell comments: 'there is a relationship of similarity between the creature and God insofar as all creatures proceed from God and must therefore in some way resemble him'. See his *Hans Urs Von Balthasar*, Continuum, 2000, p. 4.

223. See J. Fletcher, *William Temple: Twentieth-Century Christian*, Seabury Press, 1963, p. 165.

224. See W. Temple, *Christianity and Social Order*, Penguin, 1942, p. 74.

225. J. Ellul, *The Meaning of the City*, William Eerdsmans, 1970, pp. 150–1.

226. A. Davey, *Urban Christianity and Global Order: Theological Resources for an Urban Future*, SPCK, 2001, p. 61.

227. Richard Niebuhr would view these as instances of 'Christ against culture', drawing New Testament support from the book of Revelation and the First Letter of John. Support also comes from other Christian writings of the second century such as *The Epistle of Barnabas* and the *First Epistle of Clement*. See H. R. Niebuhr, *Christ and Culture*, Harper & Row, 1951, pp. 45–55.

228. A. MacIntyre, *After Virtue*, 2nd edn, Duckworth, 1985, p. 263.

229. A. Hastings, 'Cities and Gods: On Faith in the City', *The Theology of a Protestant Catholic*, SCM Press, 1990, p. 152.

230. Ward, *Cities*, p. 69.

231. Ward, *Cities*, p. 260.

232. *Changing Church*, p. 24.

233. *The Cities: A Methodist Report*, NCH Action for Children, 1997.

234. *The Cities*, pp. 55–70.

235. *The Cities*, p. 2.

236. *The Cities*, pp. 213–14. In a similar vein the first progress report on *Faith in the City* notes that 'generally speaking, Christians have had a sour view of the process of urbanization and this has been reflected in the debate about the Report'. See *Living Faith in the City: A Progress Report by the Archbishop of Canterbury's Advisory Group on Urban Priority Areas*, General Synod, 1990, p. 12, 2.6.

237. Meetings held in four cities: Newcastle, Glasgow, Cardiff and Salford. *The Cities*, p. 3.

238. More than 1,000 people completed a questionnaire. *The Cities*, p. 3.

239. *The Cities*, p. 215.

240. *The Cities*, p. 209.

241. *Staying in the City: Faith in the City Ten Years on*, Church House Publishing, 1995, p. 110 6.6.1a.

242. See L. Green, *The Challenge of the Estates: Strategies and Theology for Housing Estates Ministry*, Urban Bishops' Panel in conjunction with the National Estate Churches' Network, 1998.

243. *Faith in a Global Economy?*, Report from the Board for Social Responsibility for consideration by General Synod, document GSMISC538.

244. See Lambeth Conference Resolution 11.7 re URBANIZATION.

245. Some recent examples: (1) Hilary Russell's paper 'Shifting Sands: The Churches and the New Political Context' – given at the Centre for the Study of Theology, University of Essex, 24 February 1999; (2) 'Proclaiming the Gospel of Justice in a World of Global Capitalism', Ecumenical Conference Newman College, Birmingham, 4–5 May 1999; and (3) 'Global Capitalism and the Gospel of Justice: Politics, Economics and the UK Churches', Conference at Ushaw College, Durham, 4–7 July 2001. See also: Ward, *Cities*; Atherton, *Public Theology for Changing Times*; Davey, *Urban Christianity and Global Order*.

246. 'Clearly, man by nature is a gregarious animal born for cultivating society with other men . . . He did not give all things to one person, but some to one and some to others, so that you have need for my gifts, and I for yours. And so was born, as it were, the need for communicating necessary and useful things, which communication was not possible except in social and political life. God therefore willed that each need the service and aid of others in order that friendship would bind all together, and no one would consider another to be valueless. For if each did not need the aid of others, what would society be? What would reverence and order be? What would reason and humanity be? Everyone therefore needs the experience and contributions of others, and no one

lives to himself alone.' Cited by Johannes Althusius in his *Politica*, 1603. See new edition, Liberty Press, 1995, p. 23.

247. Issued September 1998 by the Economic Regeneration Unit of Merseyside and Region Central Ecumenical Assembly (MARCEA) as part of a submission to Liverpool Regeneration objectives.

248. Cited in *The Church Times*, 12 September 2003, p. 6.

249. *Faith & Community*, produced by the Interfaith Network for the UK with the Active Communities Unit in the Home Office. Cited in *Living Faiths in Sefton Report*, p. 9. A recent report published for the Joseph Rowntree Foundation noted the 'enormous number of projects undertaken by the Churches in the inner cities and commended their way of doing things'. R. Farnell, R. Furbey, S. Shams Al-Haqq Hills, M. Macey and G. Smith, *Faith in Urban Regeneration: Engaging Faith Communities in Urban Regeneration*, Policy Press, 2003.

250. See *Living Faiths in Sefton Report*, p. 6.

251. *Staying in the City*, p. 114.

252. *Sources of Strength and Hope: Southwell Diocesan Strategy for Urban Priority Areas*, Southwell Diocesan Social Responsibility, June 2000.

253. D. Ford and A. I. McFadyen, 'Praise', in P. Sedgwick (ed.), *God in the City: Essays and Reflections from the Archbishop of Canterbury's Urban Theology Group*, Mowbray, 1995, pp. 95–104, p. 95.

254. Grace Davie has written perceptively on this theme from a sociological perspective. See her *Religion in Britain since 1945*, Blackwell, 1994, and *Religion in Modern Europe: A Memory Mutates*, Oxford University Press, 2001. Noting the persistence of a diffused religious sense on the part of the nation in a secular age John Habgood comments: 'The common religion of the English relies heavily on concepts of fate, destiny, something to hold on to against the arbitrariness and uncertainties of life, the belief that one's number is somehow written in heaven.' See his *Confessions of a Conservative Liberal*, SPCK, 1988, p. 15.

255. *Changing Church*, p. 16, 4.1.4.

256. 'Religious institutions cannot flourish without the passive acceptance of larger numbers in the population . . . the future of religions in Europe will depend very largely on the complex relations between the two.' See G. Davie, *Religion in Modern Europe: A Memory Mutates*, Oxford University Press, 2000, pp. 80–1.

257. *Changing Church*, p. 54.

258. *Changing Church*, p. 4.

259. *Changing Church*, p. 2, 1.6. In his latest book John Atherton notes that on the basis of statistics provided by the Diocese of Manchester 'on the latter figure's projection, generously extrapolated to

a 15% decline in attendances every five years, then by 2040, the Diocesan Church will no longer exist in any significant way'. See *Marginalization*, SCM Press, 2003, p. 34.

260. Atherton, *Public Theology*, p. 85. See also *Changing Church*, p. 8, 3.1.2, and p. 26, 5.7.

261. The other report cited here is *Towards a Strategy for Church Buildings*, Manchester Diocesan Pastoral Committee, June 1998.

262. *Becoming One Body: Beyond Changing Church and Society*, Manchester Diocesan Urban Regeneration Think Tank, 8 March 2001, p. 5.

263. Extract from article by Clifford Longley, 'Now Is the Time for Church Co-operation', following the enthronement of Archbishop Cormac Murphy O'Connor as Archbishop of Westminster. *The Daily Telegraph*, 24 March 2000.

264. In Psalm 107 the city of habitation receives those spirits who have sunk, rescues the troubled, fills the hungry with good things and satisfies the thirsty.

265. For the German theologian Ernst Wolff, 'political virtue' involves looking towards 'a state or form of governance which is prepared to defend its legitimacy, its right to be obeyed and accepted, in terms of its ability not to maximise opportunities to individuals but to maximise opportunities to communities; and to do so not just by providing an abstract set of goods that everybody can bid for, but by putting resources into the educational, regenerative work that is needed to assist communities in intelligent, conversational planning about their own good that will lead to a corporately owned set of goals'. Cited by Rowan Williams in *Bevan Foundation Review*, 1, Autumn 2002, p. 42.

266. *The Guardian*, leader article, 24 September 2003.

267. Article 'Empowering the Community', *The Guardian*, 24 September 2003, p. 10.

268. 'Empowering the Community', p. 10.

269. Rowan Williams has been criticized in this respect for arguments that tend towards abstraction and general ideas rather than concrete analysis. David Martin comments: 'He thinks that there's a division of labour: the church leader's job is to spell out principles, and the politicians job is to apply them. The trouble is that, as a result, the churchman is placing in the public domain elements that the politician can't always take on board.' Cited in R. Shortt, *Rowan Williams: An Introduction*, Darton, Longman & Todd, 2003, p. 116.

270. *Faith in the City*, p.51.

271. See G. Mulgan (ed.), *Life after Politics: New Thinking for the Twenty-first Century*, Fontana Press, 1997, p. xvii.

272. P. Else, R. Farnell, R. Furbey, P. Lawless, S. Lund and

B. Wishart, *Hope in the City? The Local Impact of the Church Urban Fund*, CRESR, 1994, p. 84, 6.10.13.

273. Davey, *Urban Christianity and Global Order*, p. 39.

274. See B. Bowder, 'Use Church Know How in Inner Cities'. *Church Times*, 4 April 2003.

275. Davey, *Urban Christianity and Global Order*, p. 41.

Chapter 5

276. From M. Arnold, *East London*, cited in *Living Faith in the City*, General Synod Publications, 1990, p. 25.

277. C. G. Brown, *The Death of Christian Britain*, Routledge, 2001, p. 2.

278. See J. Atherton, *Marginalization*, SCM Press, 2003, pp. 46–7. W. H. Vanstone also comments: 'At times when the world discloses its dimension of mystery – when a hoped-for child is born or when adolescent love achieves maturity, when familiar landmarks are removed or familiar associations broken, when suffering arouses pity or terror, when bereavement takes away "part of oneself" "the services of the Church" are often sought and almost invariably welcomed; and they are welcomed, in general, *in toto*, without dilution or qualification. What is more, the probability that such need will some day arise is often recognised, especially among people of mature years, before it actually arises: one wants "the Church to be there" even if one does not need it yet.' See his 'Doctrine Diffused' essay in *Believing in the Church: The Corporate Nature of Faith*, a report by the Doctrine Commission of the Church of England, SPCK, 1981, pp. 149–54, p. 153.

279. Preface to Atherton, *Marginalization*, p. viii.

280. Mutation in a scientific sense refers to a change in genetic form in order that the species under consideration will be more suitably adapted to its environment.

281. See G. Davie, *Religion in Modern Europe: A Memory Mutates*, Oxford University Press, 2000, p. 112.

282. Words of John Henry Newman cited by I. Bradley in his *Marching to the Promised Land: Has the Church a Future?*, John Murray, 1992, p. 221.

283. See Bradley, *Marching to the Promised Land*, p. 221.

284. Reflecting on his long experience of urban mission John Vincent comments: 'We need to confirm ourselves in the areas of need . . . We need people on the ground who will express love and compassion in the face of obvious injustice and victimisation . . . We need visible examples, prophetic signs, acted parables, proleptic instances of what we want, set up for all to see . . . We need to be backyard visionaries, plucking from

the future the things that all humanity seeks, and digging in bits of them in city backyards.' See his *Into the City*, Epworth, 1982, p. 136.

285. See Edmund Burke, *Reflections on the Revolution in France*, C. C. O'Brien (ed.), Penguin, 1983, p. 135.

286. Phil. 2.1–11 is the classic New Testament text.

287. J. Moltmann, *The Church in the Power of the Spirit*, SCM Press, 1977, p. 52.

288. Part of Laurie Green, Foreword, to A. Davey, *Urban Christianity and Global Order: Theological Resources for an Urban Future*, SPCK, 2001, pp. ix–x.

289. P. Jamieson, *Living at the Edge: Sacrament and Solidarity in Leadership*, Mowbray Cassell, 1997, p. 142.

290. In trying to make sense of the city we are less prone to 'the pretension that our partial insights are complete truths that need no connection or clarification from insights elsewhere'. Cited by I. Markham, *Plurality and Christian Ethics*, rev. edn, Seven Bridges Press, 1999, p. 139.

291. Article, *The Guardian*, 6 May 2002, p. 9.

292. E. L. Graham, *Transforming Practice: Pastoral Theology in an Age of Uncertainty*, Mowbray, 1996, p. 7.

293. Martyn Percy describes this framework in terms of a 'particular way of being in the world which seeks truth and the common good in the face of a complex and fast-changing environment . . . It offers a critique of the world in a prophetic sense' yet also seeks to be a 'befriender of it'. See his 'The New Liberalism', in J. Clatworthy (ed.), *Faith for the Third Millennium*, Modern Churchpeople's Union, 1998, pp. 9–15.

294. J. Stout, *Ethics after Babel: The Languages of Morals and Their Discontents*, James Clark & Co., 1988, p. 163.

295. R. F. Thiemann, *Constructing a Public Theology: The Church in a Pluralistic Culture*, Westminster John Knox, 1991, p. 19.

296. See K. Leech, 'Ministry and Marginality', *The Sky Is Red: Discerning the signs of the Times*, Darton, Longman & Todd, 1997, pp. 225–52, pp. 247–9.

297. See J. Atherton, *Public Theology for Changing Times*, SPCK, 2000, p. 13.

298. See D. B. Forrester, *Christian Justice and Public Policy*, Cambridge University Press, 1997, p. 31.

299. Atherton, *Public Theology*, p. 2.

300. David Tracy lists these issues under the heading of 'the public of society'; the two remaining 'publics' constituting the Church and the academy. See his *The Analogical Imagination: Christian Theology and the Culture of Pluralism*, Crossroad, 1981, pp. 6–7.

301. Extract from Columbia University School of Social Work Bulletin, 1999–2000, p. 12.

302. Comment made during interview 28 October 1999. A theological endorsement of this approach is provided by C. S. Dudley, in *Basic Steps towards Community Ministry*, The Alban Institute, 1991.

303. See I. Markham, in I. Markham and Ibrahim M. Abu Rabi' (eds), *September 11: Religious Perspectives on the Causes and Consequences*, One World, 2002, p. 207.

304. See J. Blanchard, *Where Was God on September 11?*, Evangelical Press, 2002.

305. R. W. Franklin and M. S. Donovan (ed.), *Will the Dust Praise You? Spiritual Responses to 9/11*, Church Publishing, 2003.

306. Rowan Williams, *Writing in the Dust: After September 11*, Hodder & Stoughton, 2002.

307. The economist and Nobel prize winner Amartya Sen has written of 'a world with remarkable deprivation, destitution and oppression. There are many new problems as well as old ones, including persistence of poverty and unfulfilled elementary needs, occurrence of famines and widespread hunger, violation of elementary political freedoms as well as of basic liberties, extensive neglect of the interests and agency of women, and worsening threats to our environment and to the sustainability of our economic and social lives.' See his *Development as Freedom*, Oxford University Press, 2001, p. xi.

308. 'There is never any excuse for terrorism. At the same time there is an obvious need to understand the environment in which terrorism breeds.' Part of speech given by the Foreign Secretary Jack Straw to the Iranian Press. Cited in *New York Times*, 25 September 2001.

309. See P. Brierley and H. Wraight, 'Christian Leadership in a Post Modern Society' in J. Nelson (ed.), *Leading Managing Ministering: Challenging Questions for Church and Society*, Canterbury Press, 1999, p. 99.

310. See Leech, *Sky Is Red*, p. 213.

311. The presumption being made here is that the public sphere does allow the constructive contribution of theologically informed perspectives. The American theologian Ronald Thiemann has recently advanced three criteria that can serve as moral guides for public conversation between parties of differing perspectives that are required to solve matters of public import. See his *Religion in Public Life: A Dilemma for Democracy*, Georgetown University Press, 1996, pp. 135–6.

312. *Faith in the City*, pp. 185, 8.69, 187, 8.76.

313. R. Fung, *The Isaiah Vision: An Ecumenical Strategy for Congregational Evangelism*, WCC, 1992, pp. 64–5.

314. Published 12 March 1999: Correspondent Revd Geoff Wood, St Oswald's Vicarage, Lambton Road, Grove Hill, Middlesbrough TS4 2RG.

315. M. Northcott, 'Christian Futures, Postmodernity and the State of Britain', in U. King (ed.), *Faith and Praxis in a Postmodern Age*, Cassell, 1998, pp. 175–96, p. 187.

316. Northcott, 'Christian Futures', p. 187.

317. 'There has been a profound rediscovery of the doctrine of the Trinity . . . Long regarded as a rather inaccessible, though foundational doctrine, the volume of recently published work and reference has been profuse. In particular, as the House of Bishops has observed, 'in the last few decades, in the Church of England as in other churches there has been an undoubted shift towards a more thorough grounding of ecclesiology in the Trinity, together with a fresh interest in the specific action of the Holy Spirit'.

Quotation from *Mind the Gap: Integrated Continuing Ministerial Education for the Church's Ministers*, Church House Publishing, 2001, p. 14, 2.13. House of Bishops' Statement contained in *Eucharistic Presidency: A Theological Statement by the House of Bishops*, Church House Publishing, 1997, p. 13.

318. *Cities: A Methodist Report*, NCH Action for Children, 1997, p. 209.

319. Part of the theological introduction to the *Turnbull Report*, Archbishops' Commission, 1995.

320. See P. Hinchliff, 'The Church', in R. Morgan (ed.), *The Religion of the Incarnation*, Bristol Classical Press, 1989, pp. 136–58, pp. 148–9.

321. J. Zizioulas, *Being as Communion*, Darton, Longman & Todd, 1985, p. 16.

322. H. Kung, *A Global Ethic for Global Politics and Economics*, SCM Press, 1997, p. 156.

323. *Faith in the City*, p. 78, 4.25.

324. The 'Lund' principle in ecumenism.

325. 'There are two aspects of working within the churches in cities which are often undervalued. One is to do with the long haul of building networks . . . the other is to do with sustaining opportunities for church staff to meet'. See *Staying in the City: Faith in the City Ten Years On*, a report by the Bishops' Advisory Group on Urban Priority Areas, Church House Publishing, 1995, p. 104.

326. Comments made during interview, 28 October 1999.

327. Comments made during interview, 1 November 1999.

328. *Faith in the City*, p. 60, 3.26.

329. *Faith in the City*, p. 61, 3.28.

330. '[At] a time when an increasing number of spheres of human life . . . are part of a global network, no religion any longer lives in "splendid isolation". In a world where in many places people of different religions live in the same street, work in the same office and study at the

same university, what is happening in Judaism or Islam cannot be a matter of indifference to Christians. Conversely, Christians for their part will expect Jews or Muslims to formulate critically their view of the past, present and future of Christianity. In an age in which a global ecumenical consciousness has been awakened it is necessary to achieve a sense of the ecumenical, global responsibility of all for all.' Therefore 'no peace among the nations without peace among the religions. No peace among the religions without dialogue between the religions. No dialogue between the religions without investigation of the foundations of the religions.' H. Kung, *Judaism: The Religious Situation of Our Time*, SCM Press, 1992, pp. xv–xvi, p. xxii.

331. See R. L. Schreiter, *The Ministry of Reconciliation: Spirituality and Strategies*, Orbis, 1998, p. vi.

332. Ward, *Cities*, p. 257.

333. Ward, *Cities*, pp. 257–8.

334. Atherton, *Public Theology*, p. 13.

335. J. Beer, 'On Using Our Imagination in Christology', *Theology*, LXXXViii, March 1985, No. 722, pp. 89–96, p. 89.

336. M. Warnock, 'Imagination – Aesthetic and Religious', *Theology*, LXXXiii, November 1980, No. 696, pp. 403–9, p. 404.

337. D. Bonhoeffer, *Letters and Papers from Prison*, SCM Press, 1971, p. 279. Part of a letter written from Tegel, 30 April 1944.

338. A. Schweitzer, *The Quest of the Historical Jesus*, SCM Press, 1981, p. 401.

339. Col. 1.17.

340. H. Cox, *The Secular City: Secularization and Urbanization in Theological Perspective*, Penguin, 1968, p. 96, p. 264.

341. Cox, *Secular City*, p. 268.

342. 'The Greeks expressed this as *perichoresis*, meaning circularity and the inclusion of all relationships and beings.' See Atherton, *Marginalization*, p. 179.

343. Charles Gore was clear, in this respect, that Christianity is primarily a way of life. He notes that what Christ 'offers to man is not first a doctrine about God . . . to be apprehended by the intellect, and afterwards, it may be applied to life. It is the opposite. It is a way of life he teaches, a way of living to which he points man.' See his *Christ and Society*, Allan & Unwin, 1928, p. 14.

344. H. Anderson, 'Seeing the Other Whole: A Habitus for Globalisation', in P. Ballard and P. Couture (eds), *Globalisation and Difference: Practical Theology in a World Context*, Cardiff Academic Press, 1999, pp. 5–6.

345. J. D. Crossan, *Jesus: A Revolutionary Biography*, Harper Collins, 1994, p. 54.

346. See N. Ng, 'Spirituality and Theology: A Review and Perspective of Their Relationship', *Theology*, CIV, No. 818, March/April 2001, pp. 115–21, p. 119.

347. See M. Thornton, *A Joyful Heart*, SPCK, 1987, pp. 75–6, for a meditation on praying communities in the inner cities.

348. R. J. Schreiter, *Constructing Local Theologies*, Orbis, 1985, p. 17. Andrew Davey has argued that such a stance is consonant with the record of faith that shows 'how the people of God have responded to the urban environment and its wider socio-economic context, and how that encounter has been a contributing factor in the experience and understanding of community and faith'. See his *Urban Christianity and Global Order*, pp. 83–4.

349. 'The cleavage between theology and devotion is surely a fake one . . . The ugly breach between the intellectual and the affective over the centuries has done serious damage to both.' A. Jones, 'Spirituality and Theology', *Review for Religious*, 39, 1980, p. 162.

350. Ng comments: 'Concerning the relationship of spirituality and theology, Sheldrake suggests that it is like a wheel intersected by an axle. While the wheel of theology rotates around an axle of spirituality, spirituality, being three-dimensional, points outwards beyond the constraints of purely theological definition and method into another dimension. Functionally, theology offers criteria for evaluating spirituality and vice versa. On the one hand, every version of spirituality should be judged in reference to fundamental Christian beliefs like the Trinitarian God. On the other hand, spirituality unifies all attempts to approach the reality of God and offers a vital critique of any attempt by theology to launch itself into some stratosphere of timeless truth, abstract distinction or ungrounded definition.' See his 'Spirituality and Theology', pp. 120–1 and P. Sheldrake, *Spirituality and Theology*, Darton, Longman & Todd, 1998, pp. 88–95.

351. The inexorable statistics of church decline in Hull during the twentieth century are presented in P. Stubley's *A House Divided: Evangelicals and the Establishment of Hull*, Hull University Press, 1995. Relocating to Birmingham, England, after 27 years as a bishop in the Church of South India, Lesslie Newbigin has also written of the 'cold contempt for the gospel' that he encountered on doorsteps when visiting. See his autobiography *Unfinished Agenda*, SPCK, 1985, p. 249.

352. Cited by S. Bruce, *Religion in the Modern World: From Cathedrals to Cults*, Oxford University Press, 1996, p. 234.

353. Extract of a fundraising letter from the St Botolph's Project, Aldgate, London, Spring 1999.

354. See M. Clevenot, *Materialist Approaches to the Bible*, Orbis, 1985, pp. 127–8.

355. See Bruce, *Religion in the Modern World*, p. 47.

356. See Bruce, *Religion in the Modern World*, p. 46.

357. H. R. Niebuhr, *Christ and Culture*, Harper & Row, 1951, colophon edn, 1975, p. 68.

358. B. Reed, *The Dynamics of Religion: Process and Movement in Christian Churches*, Darton, Longman & Todd, 1978, p. 11.

359. M. Northcott, 'Faiths in the City', in M. Northcott (ed.), *Urban Theology: A Reader*, Cassell, 1998, pp. 314–17, p. 315.

360. See R. Beckford's *Jesus Is Dread: Black Theology and Black Culture in Britain*, Darton, Longman & Todd, 1998, for a reformulated Christology through the Rastafarian tradition in Britain that offers a Black Christ of resistance and liberation.

361. See Northcott, 'Faiths in the City', pp. 316–17.

362. See her 'Organising for Action', in M. Northcott (ed.), *Urban Theology: A Reader*, Cassell, 1998, pp. 135–7.

363. Cox, *Secular City*, p. 144. For a substantial critique of his argument, see J. Morris, 'Modernity, History and Urban Theology', *Theology*, C, No. 795, May/June 1997, pp. 194–203.

364. J. Robinson, *Truth is Two Eyed*, SCM Press, 1979.

365. Taken from L. Green, 'Blowing Bubbles: Poplar', in P. Sedgwick (ed.), *God in the City*, Mowbray, 1995, pp. 72–92, pp. 74–5.

366. The term is derived from the Latin noun 'quidditas' translating the Greek for the 'that which it is to be' of something. Commonly referred to in philosophy as the real nature or logical essence of a thing.

367. Line from Philip Larkin's poem 'Church Going', in A. S. Woodhouse, *The Poet and His Faith*, University of Chicago Press, 1965, pp. 293–4.

368. G. Steiner, *Real Presences*, Faber & Faber, 1989, p. 154.

369. Steiner, *Real Presences*, p. 156.

370. J. McGregor, *If Nobody Speaks of Remarkable Things*, Bloomsbury, 2002, p. 1.

371. McGregor, *If Nobody Speaks*, p. 2.

372. A. Ecclestone, *Yes to God*, Darton, Longman & Todd, 1975, p. 59.

373. Writing on this theme, Simone Weil comments: 'We do not obtain the most precious gifts by going in search of them but by waiting for them. Man cannot discover them by his own powers and if he sets out to seek for them he will find in their place counterfeits of which he will be unable to discern the falsity. Attention consists of suspending our thought, leaving it detached, empty and ready to be penetrated by the object, it means holding in our minds, within reach of this thought, but on a lower level and not in contact with it, the diverse knowledge we have acquired which we are forced to make use of. Above all our thought

should be empty, waiting, not seeking anything, but ready to receive in its naked truth the object which is to penetrate it.' See her *Waiting on God*, 7th edn, Collins Fontana, 1973, pp. 72–3.

374. Adapted from the 'The Prophet's Speech', in *Words from the Late, Late Service*, Glasgow, 1993.

Chapter 6

375. W. Wink, *The Powers That Be*, Doubleday, 1998, p. 187.

376. A fact that was borne out by the urban hearings described in Chapter 3.

377. 'Everywhere the question is asked about what is particular and how it can be given its own existence . . . Differences matter. We need to have roots and belong to human sized communities that give us an identity.' P. Ballard and P. Couture, 'Introduction' in P. Ballard and P. Couture (eds), *Globalisation and Difference: Practical Theology in a World Context*, Cardiff Academic Press, 1999.

378. J. V. Taylor, *The Christlike God*, SCM Press, 1992, p. 261.

379. Mark Oakley, has an interesting and amusing chapter on laughter as an integral element of the Christian life in his *The Collage of God*, Darton, Longman & Todd, 2001, pp. 86–97.

380. C. Lévi-Strauss, *The Savage Mind*, University of Chicago Press, 1966, pp. 16–36.

381. J. Stout, *Ethics after Babel: The Languages of Morals and Their Discontents*, James Clarke & Co., 1988, p. 75.

382. J. Atherton, *Public Theology for Changing Times*, SPCK, 2000, p. 96.

383. Quotation taken from a biography of Josephine Butler by E. M. Bell and cited by R. Atwell, *Celebrating the Saints: Daily Spiritual Readings to Accompany the Calendar of the Church of England*, Canterbury Press, 1998, p. 171.

384. *Faith in the City*, p. 136, 6.106.

385. K. Leech, *The Sky Is Red: Discerning the Signs of the Times*, Darton, Longman & Todd, 1997, p. 203.

386. See D. F. Ford and A. I. McFadyen, 'Praise', in P. Sedgwick (ed.), *God in the City: Essays and Reflections from the Archbishop's Urban Theology Group*, Mowbray, 1995, pp. 95–104, p. 95.

387. *Living Faith in the City*, General Synod, 1990, confines itself to issues of appropriate liturgies and the desirability of experimentation: see pp. 18–20. *Staying in the City*, Church House Publishing, 1995, includes a single reference to the task of the Church as 'being a witnessing, caring and prophetic body which worships Jesus Christ in the midst of great poverty and enormous vibrancy of human life'. See p. 98.

388. Ford and McFadyen, *God in the City*, p. 96.

389. D. W. Hardy and D. Ford, *Jubilate: Theology in Praise*, Darton, Longman & Todd, 1984, p. 85.

390. Quote attributed to Germanus, Patriarch of Constantinople (died 733).

391. Justin Martyr, *First Apology* 1, 67(<http://www.ccel.org/fathers 2/ANF-01/anf01-46. htm#P3593_620967>).

392. K. Barth, *The Word of God and the Word of Man*, Hodder & Stoughton, 1928, p. 105.

393. Barth, *Word of God*, p. 105.

394. A. Rumsey, 'The Misplaced Priest', *Theology*, CIV, No. 818, March/April 2001, pp. 102–13, p. 112.

395. D. Bonhoeffer, *Ethics*, SCM Press, 1964, p.197.

396. Ford and McFadyen, *God in the City*, p. 97.

397. 'Much of the best innovation in the provision of local health, homelessness, community regeneration and drug-related services is now being shaped by people with strong religious beliefs'. Extract from recent article from the think-tank Demos. B. Jupp, 'The Persistence of Faith', *Keeping the Faith: The New Covenant between Religious Belief and Secular Faith*, Demos, 1997. Cited in *The Church Times*, 31 March 2000.

398. Rumsey, 'Misplaced Priest', p. 112.

399. 'Praise constitutes theological reality. As a theologian, I believe that my primary theological task is praise and prayer.' Leech, *The Sky Is Red*, p. 165.

400. The French Catholic writer Charles Peguy refers to the Christian as the 'burden bearer of creation'. See A. Ecclestone, *Yes to God*, Darton, Longman & Todd, 1975, pp. 121–2.

401. L. Green, *Urban Ministry and the Kingdom of God*, SPCK, 2003, p. 143.

402. See Ford and McFadyen, 'Praise', p.97.

403. Ford and McFadyen, 'Praise', p. 97.

404. The recent work of Robin Gill is based on the European Value Systems Study Group, BBC, British Household Panel Survey and British Social Attitudes surveys. See his *Churchgoing and Christian Ethics*, Cambridge University Press, 1999.

405. Gill, *Churchgoing*, p. 225.

406. 'The imagination ranges from the very ordinary by which we see a tree as a tree, and not a vague mess of shapes and colours, by which we hear a series of sounds as a melody, to the most exalted, by which people can formulate and pass on to others, though perhaps not by the use of literal words, the vision or understanding they have.' M. Warnock, 'Imagination – Aesthetic and Religious', in *Theology*, LXXXIII, 696, November 1980, pp. 403–9, p. 405.

407. Ford and McFadyen, 'Praise', p. 98.

408. See Ford and McFadyen, 'Praise', p.98.

409. Quotation of Paul Ricoeur. See *A Ricoeur Reader*, Harvester Wheatsheaf, 1991, p. 84. In a similar vein Simone Weil comments: 'Every human being has at his roots here below a certain terrestrial poetry, a reflection of the heavenly glory . . . the link with his universal country.' See *Waiting on God*, 7th edn, Collins Fontana, 1973, p. 134.

410. Rumsey, 'Misplaced Priest', p. 110.

411. William Blake's description of the city of London. See K. Raine, *Golgonooza City of Imagination: Last Studies in William Blake*, Golgonooza Press, 1991, p. 100.

412. R. Putnam, 'Bowling Alone: America's Declining Social Capital', *Journal of Democracy*, January 1995, pp. 65–78.

413. A phrase of Alexis de Tocqueville. See his *Democracy in America*, Fontana, 1968.

414. A helpful definition of civil society is provided by Nicholas Boyle who describes it as 'all the intermediate social organizations, the autonomous and semi-autonomous institutions, the constitutional checks and balances, that lie between central government and individual citizens, that protect them from direct, and always potentially arbitrary, central interference, that give shape and substance and continuity to their lives, a focus for loyalty and a place of engagement with other citizens that is not simply an extension of the market-place – the fabric of society, in short, or, as Hegel calls it, civil society.' See his *Who Are We Now? Christian Humanism and the Global Market from Hegel to Heaney*, T&T Clark 1998, p. 18.

415. Taken from Lecture 1 available on <www.bbc.co.uk/radio4/-reith2002/lecture1>.

416. 'Sources of Christian Socialism': Lecture delivered in London, 25 March 2000.

417. Reported in *The Tablet*, 23 June 2001, p. 924.

418. T. S. Eliot 'Choruses from the Rock, 1934', *The Complete Poems and Plays of T. S. Eliot*, Faber & Faber, 1969, p. 155.

419. E. Burke, *Reflections on the Revolution in France*, Oxford University Press, 1993, p.198.

420. 'In 1991, there were over 160,000 registered charitable groups, with nearly 20% of the population engaging in some voluntary work each year, and about 10% on a weekly basis.' Atherton, *Public Theology*, p. 98.

421. See A. Shanks, *Civil Society, Civil Religion*, Blackwell, 1995, p. 7.

422. *Faith in the City*, pp. 141–2, 7.2, 7.5.

423. J. Williams, 'The Shape of the Church to Come?', *Theology*, LXXXIX, No. 729, May 1986, pp. 194–202, p. 197.

424. *Faith in the City*, p. 148, 7.32, 7.33.

425. N. Bradbury, *City of God? Pastoral Care in the Inner City*, SPCK, 1989, p. 104.

426. Atherton, *Public Theology*, pp. 96–7.

427. Shanks, *Civil Society*, p. 209.

428. R. Chartres, 'Church Ministry in London', in E. Blakebrough (ed.), *Church for the City*, Darton, Longman & Todd, 1995, pp. 28–9.

429. L. Aspinall, 'A Small Fire in the Darkness', *New Statesman*, 26 March 1999. Article based on her work for Common Purpose, an independent charity which brings people together for the purpose of improving urban communities.

430. The extensive 1990 European values study found that 53 per cent of British people regularly had the need for prayer, meditation and contemplation.

431. Robert Schreiter notes that 'if Christ's passion was redeeming for a sinful and conflicted world then perhaps my suffering can gain meaning by being united to Christ's suffering.' See his *The Ministry of Reconciliation: Spirituality and Strategies*, Orbis, 1998, pp. 4–5.

432. Margaret Walsh has written of gatherings on a council estate in Wolverhampton where: 'The people enjoy coming together. They feel relaxed and at home in one another's company . . . the scene often looks a bit chaotic to newcomers who are more used to orderly church services. Young children wander about freely . . . the occasional dog seeks admittance etc. People feel free to talk and laugh and share in the peace of Christ.' See 'Here's hoping: The Hope Community Wolverhampton', in P. Sedgwick (ed.), *God in the City*, pp. 52–71, p.66.

433. Austin Smith comments, 'for authentic inner city ministry one must cross a prepositional bridge. One must move from ministering "for" to ministering "with" the powerless of this world.' See his *Journeying with God*, Sheed & Ward, 1990, p. 112.

434. M. Northcott, 'Children' in *God in the City*, pp. 139–52, p. 151.

435. The forum was established in 1991 and met every other month at different locations in and around the city including the researcher's church, Hull University and Town Hall.

436. The slogan of *Changing Church and Society*, Manchester Diocesan Board for Church and Society, 1998, see p. 8, p. 29.

437. These included: Anchor House: an accommodation centre for people with mental health problems; Charterhouse: sheltered housing project for the elderly; Bridlington House: residential care for people moving out of larger institutions under 'care-in-the-community' provision; Housemartin Housing Association: providing accommodation and counselling for young people under 25.

438. W. E. Gladstone, *A Chapter of Autobiography*, John Murray, 1868, p. 7.

439. 'At its best, however, Christian concern for social issues is rooted in the theological convictions of creation, incarnation and redemption. It seeks to found models of civil society that reflect the renewal of citizenship, individualism and community: perhaps a place where theological traditions fuel models of equity and empowerment. Congregational life in a modest way serving as models of ecclesial polity that prefigure renewed community.' See E. L. Graham, 'Good News for the Socially Excluded? Political Theology and the Politics of New Labour', *Political Theology*, No. 2, May 2000, pp. 76–99, pp. 49–50.

440. 'It is also essential to be self-critical of structures of power and exclusion within the Church itself. Gender, homophobia, racism, moralistic judgments about family life – churches here frequently colluded with the strategies of blaming the victim and corroding self-esteem.' Graham, 'Good News for the Socially Excluded?', p. 49.

441. See *Local Strategic Partnerships Summary*, DETR, 2001, pp. 1–25.

442. During his recent address to the Churches Main Committee, the Home Secretary announced that £60,000 a year would be granted to the Inter Faith Network for a survey showing priority objectives for politicians and faith leaders working together. See *The Tablet*, 23 June 2001, p. 924.

443. Atherton, *Changing Church and World*, p. 14.

444. Boyle, *Who Are We Now?*, p. 119.

445. Comment made by Tanya Wallace during interview, 28 October 1999. For a perspective on poverty experienced by low-paid workers across America, see Barbara Ehrenreich, *Nickel and Dimed*, Granta, 2002. More recently, Polly Toynbee has provided a very readable and passionate account of what it means to live on low pay in Britain. See her *Hard Work: Life in Low Pay Britain*, Bloomsbury, 2003.

446. Part of the poem 'Weep before God', by John Wain, and cited in The Gordon Wakefield Memorial Lecture, 'A Future for Faith', given by Nigel Collinson, November 2001.

447. Humphrey Carpenter makes this point well: 'It is because of this simplicity of his teaching that Jesus has, despite all the confusions and perversions of his message over the centuries, continued to have a powerful influence on the human mind. He was not a philosopher; he did not construct any complete system of ethics; nor did he speak in moral abstractions which can be straightforwardly detached from the context of his religious beliefs. But in the manner of his teaching, his refusal to compromise when faced with any moral dilemma, his emphasis on the universality and totality, the unlimitedness of moral demands

on men, there is a force which crosses all religious barriers and appeals to us whether or not we subscribe to his religious beliefs.' See his *Jesus*, Oxford University Press, 1980, pp. 94–5.

448. William Temple taught that the basic principle of Christian ethics 'must be respect for every person simply as a person'. Quotation from *Christianity and Social Order*, and cited by R. Atwell in *Celebrating the Saints*, Canterbury Press, 1998, p. 414.

449. Sermon preached at Netherthong, 17 July 1968.

450. See article by Paul Vallely, 'How to Avoid Being a Soap Opera', *The Church Times*, 7 November 2003.

451. Green, *Urban Ministry*, p. 75.

452. Green, *Urban Ministry*, pp. 75–7.

453. Cited in R. Williams, *Ponder These Things*, Canterbury Press, 2002, p. 23.

454. Walsh, 'Here's Hoping', p. 64.

455. Cited by Atwell, *Celebrating the Saints*, p. 338.

456. Paper reprinted in *A New Christian Reader*, SCM Press, 1974, and cited by Collinson, *Future for Faith*, p. 15.

457. 'Cups'. The poem was given to me by a local poet, Ann Youle, in Hull and reflects something of what it means to believe in the city.

458. 'It seems relevant to point out that the greatest father of the Church was a black man.' E. John, in a review of H. Marrou, *St Augustine, in the Downside Review*, Spring 1958.

459. G. Wills, *Saint Augustine*, Weidenfeld & Nicolson, 1999, p. xi.

460. Wills, *Saint Augustine*, p. xi.

461. 'Augustine is the only contemporary whom we can see reacting immediately to this disaster: long sermons, closely dated, and a series of letters to leading refugees allow us to sense the complexity of his attitude. In these we can see how an event whose outline and significance tends to be taken for granted by historians, can be refracted in one participant, into a surprisingly rich spectrum. We would impoverish Augustine's reaction to the sack of Rome if we were only interested in one aspect of it, in the reaction of a Christian to the general fate of the Roman Empire. This issue rarely comes to the surface: instead, there is room in Augustine's mind for all the confused emotions of any contemporary, who feels obscurely that the world he lives in can no longer be taken for granted. We will find, in Augustine's writings of this time, perspicacious comment rubbing shoulders with the expression of political vested interest; the calculated pursuit of his own authority in an atmosphere of crisis, mingling with a mounting preoccupation with elemental themes, with guilt and suffering, old age and death.' Cited by P. Brown in *Augustine of Hippo: A Biography*, Faber & Faber, 1967, p. 290.

462. *Retractations*, 2, 43, 2. Cited in *Augustine, City of God*, D. Knowles (ed.), Pelican, 1972, pp. xv–xvi.

463. Brown, *Augustine*, p. 313.

464. Augustine, *Sermons*, 81, 8. Brown, *Augustine*, p. 298.

465. Augustine, *Sermons*, 25, 80. Cited in R. Garner, 'The Thought of St. Augustine', *Churchman*, 104. No. 4, 1990, p. 344.

466. *Augustine, City of God*, Book 4, p. 139.

467. *Augustine, City of God*, Book 1, p.35. That truth and grace are to be found in the earthly city is corroborated in the following passage from Augustine's *De Doctrina Christiana*: 'In the same way, while the heathen certainly have counterfeit and superstitious fictions in all their teachings, and the heavy burdens of entirely unnecessary labour, which every one of us must abominate and shun as we go forth from the company of the heathen under the leadership of Christ, their teachings also contain liberal disciplines which are more suited to the service of the truth, as well as a number of most useful ethical principles, and some true things are to be found among them about worshipping only the one God. All this is like their gold and silver, and not something they instituted themselves, but something which they mined, so to say, from the ore of divine providence, *veins of which are everywhere to be found.*' Cited by E. Hill, OP, in *The Works of St. Augustine for the Twenty-first Century*, New City Press, 1996, pp. 159–60.

468. *Augustine, City of God*, Book 15, pp. 21, 15.

469. Brown, *Augustine*, p. 325. See also *Augustine, City of God*, Book 19, p. 13, pp. 57–75.

470. *Augustine, City of God*, Book 12, pp. 24, 11.

471. '[A]lthough salvation has occurred, the Christian grammar of these things requires us also to say: salvation is occurring now and is still awaited, eagerly in hope'. N. Lash, 'Not Exactly Politics or Power?', *Modern Theology* 8, No. 4, 1992, p. 362.

Select Bibliography

Abel-Smith, B., and P. Townsend, *The Poor and the Poorest*, Occasional Papers in Social Administration, No. 17, G. Bell & Sons Ltd, 1965.

Anderson, H., 'Seeing the Other Whole: A Habitus for Globalisation', in P. Ballard, and P. Couture, (eds), *Globalisation and Difference: Practical Theology in a World Context*, Cardiff Academic Press, 1999.

Atherton, J., *Public Theology for Changing Times*, SPCK, 2000.

—— *Marginalization*, SCM Press, 2003.

Atwell, R., *Celebrating the Saints: Daily Spiritual Readings to Accompany the Calendar of the Church of England*, Canterbury Press, 1998.

Ayling, S., *John Wesley*, Collins, 1979.

Ballard, P., and P. Couture (eds), *Globalisation and Difference: Practical Theology in a World Context*, Cardiff Academic Press, 1999.

Barth, K., *The Word of God and the Word of Man*, Hodder & Stoughton, 1928.

Barton, S., 'Paul, Religion and Society', in S. Obelkevich, L. Roper and S. Raphael (eds), *Disciplines of Faith: Studies in Religion, Politics and Patriarchy*, Routledge & Kegan Paul, 1987, p. 170.

Becker, S., and S. MacPherson (eds), *Public Issues Private Pain: Poverty, Social Work and Social Policy*, Social Services Insight Books Care Matters Ltd, 1988.

Beckford, R., *Jesus Is Dread: Black Theology and Black Culture in Britain*, Darton, Longman & Todd, 1998.

Becoming One Body: Beyond Changing Church and Society, Manchester Diocesan Urban Regeneration Think Tank, 2001.

Believing in the Church: The Corporate Nature of Faith, a report by the Doctrine Commission of the Church of England, SPCK, 1981.

Benzeval, M., K. Judge and M. Whitehead (eds), *Tackling Inequalities in Health: An Agenda for Action*, The King's Fund, 1995.

Best, S., *Parochial Ministrations*, J. Hetchard & Son, 1839.

Blanchard, J., *Where Was God on September 11?*, Evangelical Press, 2002.

Bonhoeffer, D., *Ethics*, SCM, 1964.

—— *Letters and Papers from Prison*, SCM Press, 1971.

Boyle, N., *Who Are We Now? Christian Humanism and the Global Market from Hegel to Heaney*, T&T Clark, 1998.

Bradbury, N., *City of God? Pastoral Care in the Inner City*, SPCK, 1989.

Bradley, I., *Marching to the Promised Land: Has the Church a Future?*, John Murray, 1992.

Brierley, P., *UK Christian Handbook 2000–2001*, HarperCollins, 2000.

Brierley, P., and H. Wraight, 'Christian Leadership in a Post Modern Society', in J. Nelson (ed.), *Leading Managing Ministering: Challenging Questions for Church and Society*, Canterbury Press, 1999, pp. 85–106.

Bringing Britain Together: A National Strategy for Neighbourhood Renewal, SEU, TSO, 1998.

Brown, C. G., *The Death of Christian Britain*, Routledge, 2001.

Brown, P., *Augustine of Hippo: A Biography*, Faber & Faber, 1967.

Bruce, S., *Religion in the Modern World: From Cathedrals to Cults*, Oxford University Press, 1996.

Bryant, C., *Possible Dreams: A Personal History of the British Christian Socialists*, Hodder & Stoughton, 1997.

Burke, Edmund, *Reflections on the Revolution in France*, Oxford University Press, 1993.

Carpenter, H., *Jesus*, Oxford University Press, 1980.

Chadwick, O., *The Victorian Church*, Part 1, A. & C. Black, 1966. *The Victorian Church*, Part 2, A. & C. Black, 1970.

Changing Church and Changing Society: Developing a Strategy for Mission in the Urban Priority Areas of the Diocese of Manchester, Board for Church and Society, 1998.

Chartres, R., 'Church Ministry in London', in E. Blakebrough (ed.), *Church for the City*, Darton, Longman & Todd, 1995, pp. 25–47.

The Cities: A Methodist Report, NCH Action for Children, 1997.

Clevenot, M., *Materialist Approaches to the Bible*, Orbis, 1985.

Colson, P., *Life of the Bishop of London (Winnington-Ingram)* Jarrolds, 1935.

Cox, H., *The Secular City: Secularization and Urbanization in Theological Perspective*, Penguin, 1968.

Crossan, J. D., *Jesus: A Revolutionary Biography*, HarperCollins, 1994.

Davey, A., *Urban Christianity and Global Order: Theological Resources for an Urban Future*, SPCK, 2001.

Davidson, R., *The Character and Call of the Church of England*, Macmillan, 1912.

Davie, G., *Religion in Britain since 1945*, Blackwell, 1994.

—— *Religion in Modern Europe: A Memory Mutates*, Oxford University Press, 2001.

Dudley, C. S., *Basic Steps towards Community Ministry*, The Alban Institute, 1991.

Ecclestone, A., *Yes to God*, Darton, Longman & Todd, 1975.

Ehrenreich, B., *Nickel and Dimed*, Granta, 2002.

Ellul, J., *The Meaning of the City*, William Eerdmans, 1970.

Else, P., R. Farnell, R. Furbey, P. Lawless, S. Lund and B. Wishart, *Hope in the City? The Local Impact of the Church Urban Fund*, CRESR, 1994.

Eucharistic Presidency: A Theological Statement by the House of Bishops, Church House Publishing, 1997.

Faith in the City: A Call for Action by Church and Nation, Church House Publishing, 1985.

Farnell, R., R. Furbey, S. Shams Al-Haqq Hills, M. Macey and G. Smith, *Faith in Urban Regeneration: Engaging Faith Communities in Urban Regeneration*, Policy Press, 2003.

Fletcher, J., *William Temple: Twentieth-century Christian*, Seabury Press, 1963.

Foot, P., *London Review of Books*, 23, No. 4, 22 February 2001, p. 28.

Ford, D., 'Faith in the Cities: Corinth and the Modern City', in C. Gunton, and D. Hardy, (eds), *On Being the Church: Essays on the Christian Community*, T&T Clark, 1989, pp. 225–6.

—— 'Transformation', in P. Sedgwick (ed.), *God in the City: Essays and Reflections from the Archbishop of Canterbury's Urban Theology Group*, Mowbray, 1995, pp. 199–209.

Ford, D., and A. I. McFadyen, 'Praise', in P. Sedgwick (ed.), *God in the City: Essays and Reflections from the Archbishop of Canterbury's Urban Theology Group*, Mowbray, 1995, pp. 95–104.

Forrester, D. B., *Christian Justice and Public Policy*, Cambridge University Press, 1997.

Franklin, R. W., and M. S. Donovan (eds), *Will the Dust Praise You? Spiritual Responses to 9/11*, Church Publishing, 2003.

Friedmann, J., 'The World City Hypothesis', in P. Knox, and P. Taylor, (eds), *World Cities in a World-System*, Cambridge University Press, 1995, pp. 317–31.

Fung, R., *The Isaiah Vision: An Ecumenical Strategy for Congregational Evangelism*, WCC, 1992.

Garbett, C. F., *In the Heart of South London*, Longman, 1931.
Garner, R., 'The Thought of St. Augustine', *Churchman*, 104, 4, 1990, pp. 340–50.
Gilbert, B. B., *British Social Policy 1914–1939*, Batsford, 1970.
Gill, R., *Churchgoing and Christian Ethics*, Cambridge University Press, 1999.
Gladstone, W. E., *A Chapter of Autobiography*, John Murray, 1868.
Gore, C., (ed.), *Lux Mundi: A Series of Studies in the Religion of the Incarnation*, London, 1889.
Gore C., *Christ and Society*, Allan & Unwin, 1928.
Gorringe, T., *Capital and the Kingdom: Theological Ethics and Economic Order*, Orbis/SPCK, 1994.
Graham, E. L., *Transforming Practice: Pastoral Theology in an Age of Uncertainty*, Mowbray, 1996.
—— 'Good News for the Socially Excluded? Political Theology and the Politics of New Labour', *Political Theology*, No. 2, May 2000, pp. 76–99.
Green, L., *The Challenge of the Estates: Strategies and Theology for Housing Estates Ministry*, National Estate Churches Network, 1998.
—— 'Why Do Theological Reflection?, in M. Northcott (ed.), *Urban Theology: A Reader*, Cassell, 1998, pp. 11–18.
—— *Urban Ministry and the Kingdom of God*, SPCK, 2003.
Greenhalgh, L., and K. Worpole, 'The Convivial City', in G. Mulgan (ed.), *Life after Politics: New Thinking for the Twenty-first Century*, Fontana Press, 1997, pp. 167–76.

Habgood, J., *Confessions of a Conservative Liberal*, SPCK, 1988.
Hardy, D. W., and D. Ford, *Jubilate: Theology in Praise*, Darton, Longman & Todd, 1984.
Harrison, P., *Inside the Inner City: Life under the Cutting Edge*, Penguin, 1983.
Hastings, A., *A History of English Christianity 1920–1985*, Collins, 1986.
—— *The Theology of a Protestant Catholic*, SCM Press, 1990.
—— *Robert Runcie*, Mowbray, 1991.
Headlam, S. D., *Christian Socialism*, London, 1892.
Hicks, D. A., *Inequality and Christian Ethics*, Cambridge University Press, 2000.
Hill, E., *The Works of St. Augustine for the Twenty-first Century*, New City Press, 1996.

Hinchliff, P., 'The Church', in R. Morgan (ed.), *The Religion of the Incarnation*, Bristol Classical Press, 1989, pp. 136–58.

Hobsbawm, E., *Age of Extremes: The Short Twentieth Century 1914–1991*, Michael Joseph, 1994.

Hughes, H. P., *Social Christianity*, Hodder & Stoughton, 1890.

Inglis, K., *Churches and the Working Classes in Victorian England*, Routledge & Kegan Paul, 1963.

Iremonger, F. A., *Men and Movements in the Church: A Series of Interviews*, Longman, 1928.

Jamieson, P., *Living at the Edge: Sacrament and Solidarity in Leadership*, Mowbray Cassell, 1997.

Joseph, K., and J. Sumption, *Equality*, John Murray, 1979.

Jukes, P., *A Shout in the Street: An Excursion into the Modern City*, Faber & Faber, 1990.

Jupp, B., 'The Persistence of Faith', in *Keeping the Faith: The New Covenant Between Religious Belief and Secular Faith*, Demos, 1997.

Klein, N., *No Logo*, Flamingo, 2001.

Knowles, D. (ed.), *Augustine, City of God*, Pelican, 1972.

Kung, H., *Judaism: The Religious Situation of Our Time*, SCM Press, 1992.

——*A Global Ethic for Global Politics and Economics*, SCM Press, 1997.

Landry, C., *The Creative City: A Toolkit for Urban Innovators*, Earthscan, 2000.

Lash, N., 'Not Exactly Politics or Power?', *Modern Theology*, 8, No. 4, 1992, p. 362.

Leech, K., *Struggle in Babylon: Racism in the Cities and Churches of Britain*, Sheldon Press, 1988.

——*The Sky Is Red: Discerning the Signs of the Times*, Darton, Longman & Todd, 1997.

Living Faith in the City, General Synod Publications, 1990.

Living Faith in the City: A Progress Report by the Archbishop of Canterbury's Advisory Group on Urban Priority Areas, General Synod, 1990.

Living Faiths in Sefton Report, Diocese of Liverpool and Sefton Council for Voluntary Services, 2002.

Local Strategic Partnerships Summary, DETR, 2001.

Lockhart, J. G., *Cosmo Gordon Lang*, Hodder & Stoughton, 1949.

Lovering, J., 'Global Restructuring and Local Impact', in M. Pacione (ed.), *Britain's Cities: Geographies of Division in Urban Britain*, Routledge, 1997, pp. 15–28.

The Lowry Centre: A Project for the Millennium, Salford City Council, 1996.

McGregor, J., *If Nobody Speaks of Remarkable Things*, Bloomsbury, 2002.

MacIntyre, A., *After Virtue*, 2nd edn, Duckworth, 1985.

Markham, I., *Plurality and Christian Ethics*, rev. edn, Seven Bridges Press, 1999.

Markham, I., in Markham, I., and Abu Rabi', I. M. (eds), *September 11: Religious Perspectives on the Causes and Consequences*, One World, 2002, pp. 206–28.

Massey, D., *Space, Place and Gender*, Polity Press, University of Minnesota Press, 1994.

Massey, D., J. Allen and S. Pile, *City Worlds*, Routledge, 1999.

Maurice, F. D., *The Kingdom of Christ*, 1838, Everyman edn, n.d.

—— *On the Reformation of Society and How All Classes May Contribute to It*, Forbes & Knibb, 1851.

Meeks, W., *The First Urban Christians: The Social World of the Apostle Paul*, Yale University Press, 1983.

Mind the Gap: Integrated Continuing Ministerial Education for the Church's Ministers, Church House Publishing, 2001.

Moltmann, J., *The Church in the Power of the Spirit*, SCM Press, 1977.

Monbiot, G., *Captive State: The Corporate Take Over of Britain*, Macmillan, 2000.

Mulgan, G. (ed.), *Life after Politics: New Thinking for the Twenty-first Century*, Fontana Press, 1997.

National Strategy for Neighbourhood Renewal: A Framework for Consultation, SEU, 2000.

Nevins, A. (ed.), *Diary of John Quincy Adams 1794–1845*, Charles Scribner's Sons, 1951.

A New Commitment to Neighbourhood Renewal: National Strategy Action Plan, Social Exclusion Unit, 2001.

Newbigin, L., *Unfinished Agenda*, SPCK, 1985.

Newman, J. H., *Sermons, chiefly on the theory of Religious Belief preached before the University of Oxford*, 2nd edn, Rivington, 1884.

Niebuhr, R. H., *Christ and Culture*, Harper & Row, 1951.

Norman, E. R., *Church and Society in England 1770–1970*, Oxford University Press, 1976.

Northcott, M., 'Children', in P. Sedgwick (ed.), *God in the City: Essays and Reflections from the Archbishop of Canterbury's Urban Theology Group*, Mowbray, 1995, pp. 139–52.

—— 'Christian Futures, Postmodernity and the State of Britain', in U. King (ed.), *Faith and Praxis in a Postmodern Age*, Cassell, 1998, pp. 175–96.

Northcott, M. (ed.), *Urban Theology: A Reader*, Cassell, 1998.

Oakley, M., *The Collage of God*, Darton, Longman & Todd, 2001.

O'Brien, C. (ed.), *Reflections on the Revolution in France*, Penguin, 1983.

O'Donnell, J., *Hans Urs Von Balthasar*, Continuum, 2000.

O'Hear, A., *After Progress: Finding the Old Way Forward*, Bloomsbury, 1999.

O'Loughlin, J., 'Between Sheffield and Stuttgart: Amsterdam in an Integrated Europe and a Competitive World Economy', in L. Deben, W. Heinemeijer and D. van der Vaart (eds.), *Understanding Amsterdam: Essays on Economic Vitality, City Life and Urban Form*, Het Spinuis, 1993.

Our Towns and Cities: The Future. Delivering an Urban Renaissance, DETR, The Stationery Office, 2000.

Paget, S., *Henry Scott Holland*, John Murray, 1921.

Percy, M., 'The New Liberalism', in J. Clatworthy (ed.), *Faith for the Third Millennium*, Modern Churchpeople's Union, 1998.

Powerful Whispers, Bradford Faith in the City Forum, 1995.

Preston, R., *Church and Society in the Late Twentieth Century*, SCM Press, 1983.

—— 'A Bishop Ahead of His Church', in R. J. Elford and I. S. Markham (eds), *The Middle Way: Theology, Politics and Economics in the Late Thought of R. H. Preston*, SCM Press, 2000, pp. 21–9.

—— 'Not out of the Wood Yet', in R. J. Elford and I. S. Markham (eds), *The Middle Way: Theology, Politics and Economics in the Late Thought of R. H. Preston*, SCM Press, 2000, pp.85–90.

Raban, J., *God, Man and Mrs Thatcher*, Chatto & Windus, 1989.

Raine, K., *Golgonooza City of Imagination: Last Studies in William Blake*, Golgonooza Press, 1991.

Ramsey, M., *Durham Essays and Addresses*, SPCK, 1956.

—— *From Gore to Temple: The Development of Anglican Theology between Lux Mundi and the Second World War 1889–1939*, Longman, 1960.

Reed, B., *The Dynamics of Religion: Process and Movement in Christian Churches*, Darton, Longman & Todd, 1978.

Robinson, J., *Truth Is Two Eyed*, SCM Press, 1979.

Robson, B., *Assessing the Impact of Urban Policy*, HMSO, 1994.

Rogers, R., and A. Power, *Cities for a Small Country*, Faber & Faber, 2000.

Rumsey, A., 'The Misplaced Priest', *Theology*, CIV, No. 818, March/April 2001, pp. 102–13.

Russell, H. (ed.), *The Servant Church in Granby*, Centre for Urban Studies, University of Liverpool, 1989.

Russell, H., *Poverty Close to Home: A Christian Understanding*, Mowbray, 1995.

Sacks, J., *The Dignity of Difference: How to Avoid the Clash of Civilizations*, Continuum, 2002.

Sandercock, L., *Towards Cosmopolis – Planning for Multicultural Cities*, John Wiley & Sons, 1998.

Sassen, S., *The Global City: London, New York and Tokyo*, Princeton University Press, 1991.

Schreiter, R. L., *Constructing Local Theologies*, Orbis, 1985.

—— *The Ministry of Reconciliation: Spirituality and Strategies*, Orbis, 1998.

Schweitzer, A., *The Quest of the Historical Jesus*, SCM Press, 1981.

Seeds of Hope in the Parish, Church House Publishing, 1996.

Sen, A., *Development as Freedom*, Oxford University Press, 2001.

Shanks, A., *Civil Society, Civil Religion*, Blackwell, 1995.

Sheldrake, P., *Spirituality and Theology*, Darton, Longman & Todd, 1998.

Sheppard, D., *Bias to the Poor*, Hodder & Stoughton, 1983.

Short, J. R., *The Urban Order*, Blackwell, 1996.

Shortt, R., *Rowan Williams: An Introduction*, Darton, Longman & Todd, 2003.

Smith, A., *Journeying with God*, Sheed & Ward, 1990.

Socio-demographic Change and the Inner City, DOE, 1995.

Sources of Strength and Hope: Southwell Diocesan Strategy for Urban Priority Areas, Southwell Diocesan Social Responsibility, 2000.

Staying in the City: A Report of the Bishops' Advisory Group on Urban Priority Areas, Church House Publishing, 1995.

Steiner, G., *Real Presences*, Faber & Faber, 1989.

Stout, J., *Ethics after Babel: The Languages of Morals and Their Discontents*, James Clark & Co., 1988.

Stranks, C. J., *Dean Hook*, Mowbray 1954.

Strauss, C. L., *The Savage Mind*, University of Chicago Press, 1966.

Stubley, P., *A House Divided: Evangelicals and the Establishment of Hull*, Hull University Press, 1995.

Taylor, J. V., *The Christlike God*, SCM Press, 1992.

Temple, W., *Christianity and Social Order*, Penguin, 1942.

Theissen, G., *The Social Setting of Pauline Christianity: Essays on Corinth*, T&T Clark; Fortress Press, 1983.

Thiemann, R. F., *Constructing a Public Theology: The Church in a Pluralistic Culture*, Westminster John Knox, 1991.

——— *Religion in Public Life: A Dilemma for Democracy*, Georgetown University Press, 1996.

Thompson, G., 'Economic Globalization?', in D. Held (ed.), *A Globalizing World? Culture, Economics, Politics*, Routledge, 2000, p. 105.

Thornton, M., *A Joyful Heart*, SPCK, 1987.

Townsend, P. (ed.), *The Concept of Poverty*, Heinemann, 1970.

Townsend, P., *Poverty in the United Kingdom: A Survey of Household Resources and Standards of Living*, Allen Lane Penguin Books Ltd., 1979.

Townsend, P., N. Davidson and M. Whitehead (eds), *Inequalities in Health: The Black Report: The Health Divide*, Penguin, 1990.

Toynbee, P., *Hard Work: Life in Low-pay Britain*, Bloomsbury, 2003.

Tracy, D., *The Analogical Imagination: Christian Theology and the Culture of Pluralism*, Crossroad, 1981.

Unemployment and the Future of Work: An Enquiry for the Churches, CCBI, 1997.

Van Drimmelen, R., *Faith in a Global Economy: A Primer for Christians*, WCC Publications, 1998.

Vincent, J., *Into the City*, Epworth, 1982.

——— 'Wanted – an Urban Theology', in P. Sedgwick (ed.), *God in the City: Essays and Reflections from the Archbishop of Canterbury's Urban Theology Group*, Mowbray, 1995.

Walsh, M., 'Here's Hoping: The Hope Community, Wolverhampton', in P. Sedgwick (ed.), *God in the City: Essays and Reflections from the Archbishop of Canterbury's Urban Theology Group*, Mowbray, 1995, pp. 52–71.

Ward, G., *Cities of God*, Routledge, 2000.

Warnock, M., 'Imagination – Aesthetic and Religious', *Theology*, LXXXIII, 696, 1980, pp. 403–9.

——— *A Memoir: People and Places*, Duckworth, 2000.

Weber, M., *The Protestant Ethic and the Spirit of Capitalism*, Unwin, 1985.

Weil, S., *Waiting on God*, 7th edn, Collins Fontana, 1973.

Wickham, E. R., *Church and People in an Industrial City*, Lutterworth 1957.

Wilkinson, A., *Christian Socialism: Scott Holland to Tony Blair*, SCM Press, 1998.

Williams, J., 'The Shape of the Church to Come', *Theology*, LXXXiX, 729, May 1986, pp. 194–202.

Williams, R., *Ponder These Things*, Canterbury Press, 2002.

—— *Writing in the Dust: After September 11*, Hodder & Stoughton, 2002.

Willmer, H., 'Images of the City and the Shaping of Humanity', in A. Harvey (ed), *Theology in the City*, SPCK, 1989, pp. 32–46.

Willmott, P. (ed.), *Urban Trends 2: A Decade in Britain's Deprived Urban Areas*, Policy Studies Institute, 1994.

Willmott, P., and R. Hutchinson (eds), *Urban Trends 1: A Report on Britain's Deprived Urban Areas*, Policy Studies Institute, 1992.

Wills, G., *St Augustine*, Weidenfeld & Nicolson, 1999.

Wilson, A. N., *The Victorians*, Hutchinson, 2002.

Wink, W., *The Powers That Be*, Doubleday, 1998.

Woodhouse, A. S., *The Poet and His Faith*, University of Chicago Press, 1965.

Wright, N. T., 'The Letter to the Galatians: Exegis and Theology', in J. B. Green and M. Turner (eds), *Between Two Horizons: Spanning New Testament Studies and Systematic Theology*, W. B. Eerdmans, 2000.

Zizioulas, J., *Being as Communion*, Darton, Longman & Todd, 1985.

Subject Index